Most of us don't know how to grieve well. When dark days or long seasons of disappointment knock on the door of our own lives — and they will — we will need more than clichés, advice, or the surface-level "thoughts and prayers" of those around us. And that's why I am so thankful Drew wrote *Invisible Grief*. This book is compe''   '' ' '   ''' hope. In these pages you will    truth, but also the warmth of   'erience. Drew writes as a frier   w near to Jesus through the hå   he Savior sees us, loves us, str   ough them all.

Adam Ramsey
Lead Pastor, Liberti Church, Gold Coast, Australia;
Director for Acts 29 Asia Pacific

Drew writes from a place of experience—a trusted guide who has been through the fires of heartache and returned to share wisdom to all who will hear. Rather than burying the pain of the past, he encourages us to face it fiercely and find the One who walks with us through our darkest valleys.

AJ Sherrill
Lead Pastor, Saint Peters Church,
Mount Pleasant, South Carolina

Invisible Grief is the book I wish I had on my nightstand during my own painful season of unrealized dreams and unanswered prayers. The truths Drew has penned on these pages will put language to your experience, offer comfort beyond the clichés, and point you to an enduring hope that you can trust. This book will be my first recommendation and go-to gift for loved ones in my life who find themselves facing the painful reality of invisible grief. Thank you, Drew for this special resource!

Nicole Zasowski
Licensed marriage and family therapist;
author, *What If It's Wonderful?*

Sometimes grief and pain are so deep that we want to run from it. Drew Hensley, in this refreshingly honest and life changing book, says that we should go there anyway. Why is that? That's because that's where God meets his people … in the dark places. This is a profound book that changes everything about the places we all lament. Read it and share it with everyone you love!

Steve Brown
Founder of Key Life Network;
author, *A Scandalous Freedom*

Invisible Grief is a tender, courageous invitation to name and walk through the ache of what never was—the silent sorrow so many carry in secret. Drew Hensley writes with raw honesty and deep pastoral wisdom, offering the kind of empathic presence that gives language to lament and makes space for healing. This book is a gift for those whose losses defy categories but not God's compassionate witness.

Chuck DeGroat
Professor of Pastoral Care and Christian Spirituality, Western Theological Seminary, Holland, Michigan

Grief is usually a shared experience. And although that sharing doesn't make the pain go away, knowing that others are with us in it does lessen the burden and quells the question, "Am I alone?" But what about the grief that is unseen … invisible? In this deeply transparent and biblically faithful book, you'll find the answer you're looking for. Far from trite superficialities, *Invisible Grief* offers soul-comforting truth about the Suffering Savior who loves you and assures you that though others may not see your heartbreak, he sees it all.

Elyse Fitzpatrick
Speaker and author, *Because He Loves Me*

AN HONEST CONVERSATION ON THE PAIN AND LOSS
OF UNREALIZED HOPES, DREAMS, AND GOOD DESIRES

INVISIBLE GRIEF

DREW HENSLEY

FOREWORD BY JUSTIN S. HOLCOMB

CHRISTIAN
FOCUS

Copyright © Drew Hensley 2026

print ISBN 978-1-5271-1347-3
ebook ISBN 978-1-5271-1407-4

10 9 8 7 6 5 4 3 2 1

Published in 2026
Christian Focus Publications Ltd,
Geanies House, Fearn, Ross-shire,
IV20 1TW, Scotland.

www.christianfocus.com

Cover design by Drew Hensley

Printed and bound by Bell & Bain, Glasgow

*To Laura and Silas who I love beyond words.
Outside of Jesus, you are the very best gift this life
has to offer.*

*"Always remember there was nothing worth sharing
like the love that let us share our name."*
—*The Avett Brothers*

*To all of those who walked with me and Laura
through our deepest grief, you will never know how
much your love and care have meant to us.*

*A special thanks to Jonathan Hiott for
his assistance with structure and story.*

CONTENTS

Foreword ix
Introduction 1

WHAT WE LAY DOWN

1   The Temptation to Run 9
2   The Lies We Believe 29
3   Does God Really Care? 47

WHAT WE PICK UP

4   It's Okay to Not Be Okay 65
5   The Gift of Grief 79
6   A Better Identity 89
7   Purpose and Promise 109

A Letter to Silas 137

HOW WE MOVE FORWARD

8   In Gospel Community 141
9   In Joy and Grief 157

Epilogue: Helping the Hurting 181
Notes 189

FOREWORD

Grief is a universal experience—one that has touched us all in some form, whether through the loss of loved ones, dreams, or even the intangible hopes that once buoyed us through life. Yet, for many of us, there is a specific type of grief that often goes unseen and unnamed: the grief of what never was and what may never be. It is a quiet sorrow, an ache that resides in the shadowy corners of our hearts, often unnoticed by others but deeply felt by us. Drew Hensley calls this "invisible grief," and in his book he courageously brings it to light.

The reality of invisible grief resonates with a profound biblical truth: God sees our suffering, even when others do not. The Scriptures remind us repeatedly of God's intimate awareness of our pain. The psalmist writes, "The LORD is near to the brokenhearted and saves the crushed in spirit" (Ps. 34:18). This nearness of God is neither abstract nor distant; it is the tender, compassionate presence of a God who knows what it means to grieve. As Drew shares his journey and the journeys of others, inviting us into their experiences of loss, he also draws us closer to the one who has carried our sorrows and borne our griefs (Isa. 53:4).

This book is a gift for anyone who has felt the sting of unmet desires, unrealized dreams, or unanswered prayers. Drew writes with honesty and vulnerability—not from a place of theory but of lived experience—naming the questions many of us have whispered in our darkest moments: Does God see me? Does He care? Why hasn't He answered this good and godly prayer? These questions are not foreign to Scripture. In fact, the Bible is filled with examples of men and women crying out to God with raw, unfiltered honesty. Job's lament, the psalms of complaint, and Jesus' own cry of dereliction on the cross remind us that bringing our grief to God is not a sign of faithlessness but of trust.

In my own reflections on grief, I have been struck by how often we are tempted to minimize or deny our pain. We live in a culture that values strength, independence, and efficiency, leaving little room for the slow, messy process of mourning. Drew reminds us that invisible grief—and all grief, for that matter—does not follow a predictable timeline. It cannot be hurried, nor should it be. Instead, he writes, we are invited to slow down, lament, and face our pain with honesty and courage.

This honesty is essential because it is only in acknowledging our grief that we can experience the depth of God's compassion. In Exodus, we read that "God heard their groaning, and God remembered his covenant…God saw the people of Israel—and God knew" (Exod. 2:24-25). This same God hears, sees, and knows your grief. He does not dismiss or belittle it. Instead, He mourns with you, standing in solidarity with your pain through Jesus Christ, who was "a man of sorrows and acquainted with grief" (Isa. 53:3).

One of the most powerful aspects of Drew's book is his insistence that grief is not a problem to be solved but a reality to be faced. This is a profoundly countercultural message. We often hear well-meaning but unhelpful platitudes, like "time heals all wounds" or "God must have a reason." Drew dismantles these myths with grace and truth, offering instead the hope of the gospel. He reminds us that while our grief is real, it is not ultimate. Resurrection is. In the words of Jesus, "Blessed are those who mourn, for they shall be comforted" (Matt. 5:4).

Grief, as Drew so beautifully articulates, is not something we endure alone. The Christian faith offers us the gift of community—a gospel-centered fellowship where we can bear one another's burdens and find encouragement in our shared hope. This communal aspect of healing is woven throughout Drew's reflections, and it is a crucial reminder that we are not meant to walk through grief in isolation. Just as the body of Christ shares in one another's joys, so too do we share in one another's sorrows.

But even more profound than the fellowship of believers is the fellowship we have with Christ in our suffering. Hebrews 4:15 assures us that "we do not have a high priest who is unable to sympathize with our weaknesses, but one who in every respect has been tempted as we are, yet without sin." Jesus' solidarity with us in our grief is not merely empathetic; it is redemptive. He entered into our suffering so that He might ultimately conquer it. Because of His death and resurrection, we can grieve with hope, knowing that our tears will one day be wiped away and death itself will be no more (Rev. 21:4).

Drew's words are tender and pastoral, offering a balm for wounded hearts. His transparency about his own journey through infertility and unmet desires creates a space for readers to reflect on their own stories of loss. This book does not shy away from the hard questions or the uncomfortable realities of grief. Instead, it points us to the compassionate heart of God, who meets us in our sorrow and promises to bring beauty from ashes.

As you read this book, may you find permission to grieve honestly, to lament boldly, and to hope expectantly. Drew's journey and the stories of those he has encountered along the way are a reminder that while grief may feel like an uninvited guest who has overstayed its welcome, it is not without purpose. In the hands of our Redeemer, even our pain can be transformed into something beautiful. My prayer for you is that you would encounter the God who sees you, knows you, and loves you—even in the midst of your invisible grief.

Justin S. Holcomb
Bishop, Episcopal Diocese of Central Florida

INTRODUCTION

I pulled off to the side of the road by Greenlake Park in
Seattle. As the misting rain hit the windshield, I broke
down in uncontrollable tears. While I could see young
children playing soccer as parents stood nearby, I felt—but
could not see—the deep ache and sorrow that had become
all too familiar. While some forms of grief are the result
of someone's death or injury, or become present when
something is gone or lost, this is different. This kind of grief,
this invisible grief, rushes in because of something we desire
but are not given, a pain that is birthed from what has never
been and may never be.

This feeling can be like an uninvited guest that you
expected to stay for only a day or two at most, but has now
become an incorrigible roommate you can't seem to get rid
of. And if that wasn't bad enough, this "roommate" seems to
hold a certain power that's hard to explain and most don't
understand. When you try to describe it to others, it's hard to
put a finger on. It's not just grief, it's invisible grief—a deep-
seated reminder of what has never been and may never be.

For my wife, Laura, and me, this roommate had made a home in our lives for the past seven long years. Seven years of trying to conceive a child. Seven years of tried and failed surgeries. Seven years of watching others have children, watching them move ahead while we felt stuck in a sick and twisted time warp. Yes, seven long years of riding the month-in- month-out roller-coaster of "cross-your-fingers with eyes closed" type hope, only to be met with another gray cloud of disappointment and a new bitter dose of discouragement. What made things even harder is that we knew our desires were good. We knew what we spent countless nights praying and pleading with God for was something He actually tells us is a good thing: "be fruitful and multiply" (Gen. 1:28). So why not us? Why not answer this prayer? Why not fill our home with the laughter of children running around instead of this deafening, defeated silence? Although our questions felt like they were going into an old, dusty comment box that no one ever checked, it got better over time. As they say, "time heals all wounds." After enough time passed, so did the grief...right? No. Not to be a Debbie Downer but it wasn't like that at all. Let me explain.

When I was eleven my grandfather died; it was the first time I came face to face with death and this thing called "grief." I obviously didn't understand everything that was happening, but I did understand that I had lost something—more than that, someone—that I really loved. It was a sad time for me and my family, but there were also fond memories that couldn't be taken away; there was a life well lived; there was sadness that my grandfather was gone in the earthly sense, but also peace and hope that came with knowing we would be united again in eternity.

When it comes to invisible grief and the grief my wife and I felt (and feel) towards infertility, peace and understanding are not things we can even begin to wrap our heads around. Why? Because there are no memories to think back on, no flesh and bones body to say goodbye to, no hope of seeing them again when I breathe my last because they never breathed their first. The dreams of children that share my DNA, nose, eyes, traits, will never exist. I would argue that this type of "invisible grief," the death of hopes, dreams, and desires, is just as painful as any other human loss—if not more so. When approaching grief, many psychologists look through the lens of tangible loss of health or life. Based on this metric, researchers have found that "Prolonged grief is relatively rare experienced by about 10 percent of the bereaved."[1] While this is true for those who have lost someone, it's not very helpful when it comes to the death of what never was.

Unfortunately, invisible grief doesn't come with a timer. In fact, the longer this season dragged on, the louder and heavier the grief became and along with it raw, unfiltered, brutally honest questions. Is there anyone there? God, do you even care about us? Did we do something to cause this? Are you angry with us? Are you really a good and loving God, because it sure doesn't feel like it? Am I the only one who feels this way? Is something wrong with me?

Have you found yourself there? Do you find yourself here right now? Or maybe you know someone who's living through and enduring the grief of what has never been and may never be. Invisible grief is the product of pain and loss that comes in many forms. For us, our sorrow was birthed out of infertility. For you or someone you know it might be mental or emotional health challenges that prevent healthy relationships or pursuits, singleness where there is a desire to be married, abandonment and feeling the weight of those missing relationships and memories, a physical limitation that feels like it's taken your future captive, and the list goes on.

Essentially, the sorrow that accompanies any good hope, dream, or desire that hasn't come to life, or has died because it never existed, we will define as "invisible grief." But hear this…you're not alone. I know it might feel like it, and I also know this isn't a common subject or something the Christian community has really embraced or figured out how to approach. It's somewhat awkward and doesn't fit in the traditional box of "loss." But there are many walking this out. You might not know their names and you might not ever see their faces, but just like you and me, they're looking for hope in the dark. That may be why you picked up this book and it's the whole reason I decided to write it. Not because I have a PhD in the subject matter of grief, but because I've been there, sometimes I'm still there, and I don't want you to take this journey alone.

WHY ANOTHER BOOK ON GRIEF?

This is a great question and one I pondered for years. My hope in writing this is to provide new language and perspective to a form of grief that often gets passed over and even repressed. I'm tired of watching so many people struggle in silence, unsure if their grief is valid or worth someone else's time and attention (it is!). I believe invisible grief is unique enough from how we traditionally think about the topic that we could use a different approach. This book represents what Laura and I looked for but couldn't find: an honest conversation about the pain and loss from what never was and may never be, feelings that were, at times, hard to fully describe. Let me say at the start, that this book isn't going to give you all of the answers you're looking for because, in reality, none of us have all the answers to remedy this type of pain, loss, and sorrow. This book also isn't going to offer "five ways to a better tomorrow" as if that ever really works. You also won't find any Christian platitudes here, no "God is closing a door but opening a window" or any of that nonsense that only serves as a placebo to what our heart really needs and desires: hope and healing in what most likely is the most painful part of your life.

Throughout these pages we're going to spend time considering both this invisible form of grief and the visible, beautiful gospel of Jesus. We'll look at a healthy approach to this kind of grief. We'll look to unearth and dismantle the lies about grief which we have been fed, and look to replace those with the truth of God's ability, His presence, His plans, and His goodness. We'll spend time being honest about the tension between faith and doubt, and between pain, purpose, and promise. And yes, we will rebuild. We will rebuild and redefine, not on our feelings, but on the truth of the gospel and how this good news changes everything. We will walk through biblical examples, personal stories, and Jesus' own words to help build back what's been broken down. We will rebuild and redefine identity, and we will consider what it means to live with both joy and sorrow, the importance of community, and what hope looks like as we move forward. Truth will be essential to this conversation because, at the end of the day, that's the foundation where we need to plant our feet.

I hope you don't see this book as a lecture or detached theory but more of an invitation into the living room to have an honest, heartfelt conversation with a pastor and friend who has been there and continues to be there.

There's an obvious love-hate relationship in writing this book. While I hate that I'm able to talk about this because of the grief experienced, and I hate that you're in a position to pick up and read a book like this, I also love that in all of the brokenness and bitterness this world can throw at us, we don't have to go through it alone. I love that although the grief we feel may be invisible, God's desire to meet us here and offer authentic hope isn't. Maybe this feels like a pipe dream right now or you feel too worn out to hope again—I get it. I really, really get it. If you feel like this now or feel like this at any time walking through this book, please know that I'll be hoping for you and with you. When you feel like your faith is drying up, borrow some of mine just as I've had to borrow from others along the way. There is hope—real, lasting, unchanging hope that even the darkest night can't hide and the longest day can't outlast.

Whether you are reading this alone or with a group, I consider it an honor that you would allow me to share our story and the stories of others with you, I really mean that. Your grief is not lost on me just as I trust my grief will not be lost on you. My hope is that this honest conversation will provide clarity, encouragement, fresh perspective, new language, and a lens through which to view and interact with your grief. But my greatest hope is that you experience the unmistakable and unavoidable love of Jesus. A love that tends to your wounds and gently reminds that you are not "less than." One that assures you that your pain is seen, your sorrow is known, and you are never abandoned. A love that promises good for you. A love that, through the pain, through the loss, through the waiting, takes you by the hand, wipes away your tears, cleans your face, and says, "Know that you are not alone and, my deeply loved child, your grief is not wasted." This is my greatest hope, because, through it all, this is our greatest need.

PART 1

WHAT WE LAY DOWN

WHAT WE SAY NOW

1

THE TEMPTATION TO RUN

When I was in high school I ran distance track, mainly the one and two mile races. There was something about running I fell in love with and it helped keep me in shape for basketball season. My favorite movie at the time was *Prefontaine* starring Jered Leto. It was a biopic on Steve Prefontaine, this kid who grew up trying to excel at every sport imaginable only to find himself too short, or too skinny, until he started running. Even though he had one leg longer than the other and a self-admitted odd stride, he was the epitome of drive and determination in the sixties and seventies. Nothing would get in the way of him attending the top track school in the country, the University of Oregon, and subsequently making the Olympics. He was a force to be contended with until his untimely death in a car accident at the age of twenty-four.[1] I was no Prefontaine, but I did love a good run.

Occasionally on the weekend I would run with a friend from church named Jim. Our city track club would put on 5k's, 10k's, and from time to time longer races. I was sixteen years old, weighed eighty pounds less than I do now, and ran on average five miles a day. I had a mile time of four minutes and fifty-two seconds, so when it came to running the annual cheese and sauerkraut ten-mile race, I felt pretty confident. This was a unique race because you would first guess what you believed your finishing time would be. The person closest got a giant block of cheese and the person furthest from their time got, along with shame, sauerkraut. Now that you have some background, let's move to the race. We all take off and, per usual, the first few miles are a breeze. I took off quickly as I wanted to shoot for a personal best on the average time of each mile. I was convinced that I could keep a fast pace for all ten miles. Here's the problem, I averaged five miles a day, not ten. Once I hit mile eight, my legs turned to Jell-O. I kid you not, on mile number nine as I made my way toward the finish at literally a snail's pace— yes, I said literally—a ninety-year-old man passed me. I was completely worn out and couldn't believe I even finished the race. This was, by no stretch of anyone's imagination, the most humbling experience of my first sixteen years as I left that day with a giant jar of sauerkraut. My fast-paced, sprint mentality let me down. Simply telling myself "you can do this" wasn't enough. As I walked back to the car what came with me was newfound respect and understanding for how to approach this lengthy race.

There are many ways we could start this conversation as we look to navigate invisible grief, no matter what form that's taken in your life or in the life of someone you know. With that in mind, I keep circling back to the need for us to start with *how* before *what*. Obviously we already know *what* we're going to talk about, but *how* we're going to do this can't be flippantly passed over or assumed. From my own experience, I absolutely believe that when it comes to something so deeply personal and heavy, if this endeavor is worth taking, if this lengthy conversation is worth having, we must start the right way and with the right posture and expectations for any of this to be truly helpful and hopeful. I can't overstress this point. The reason I can't overstress this is because it's something I struggled with for years, and on occasion I still miss the direct object.

I'm going to warn you now that I love music. Like I listen to music throughout the entire day kind of love, sometimes the same album or song on repeat for hours like I'm doing right now as I type these words. My wife Laura *loves* it. (Yes, that's sarcasm.) Throughout my life, and in different seasons, I've found that certain songs are able to articulate what I'm feeling in a way that's deeply comforting, especially when I can't put my own words to the emotions I'm feeling. With that, I want to share some lyrics from the song "Illusion" from the album *Fear* by Citizens, led by my good friend Zach Bolen. Zach and I served together in Seattle and I have always appreciated his desire to write music that authentically captures the human experience and connects it to the gospel and faith in a way that's not shoe-horned or piffy. See if you can relate to what this song says:

> In an empty room
> Inside a haunted house I waste, away
> Nothing getting in
> There's nothing coming out I fade to grey
> All the memories I've been pushing out of my head
> I need to face the pain, I never did
> But if I open this door I won't really know what's ahead
> I don't know how to feel, afraid to live
>
> Running from the heartbreak of the night
> It's an illusion of a life
> I tremble with desire
> Strangling the grief out of the light
> It's an illusion of a life
> I long to feel the fire[2]

Can you relate? I could: I still can. We will be tempted to run, and that run will take on many different forms. We will be tempted to run *from* our grief—hoping that if we can run fast enough and far enough the grief will cease to exist—but when we turn around, there it is. We will be tempted to try and run *through* our grief to quick fixes (self-help that turns out to be anything but helpful), trying to rush and turn a wound into a scar overnight, only to find that we've made the wound even bigger. We will be tempted to run to unhealthy places to *numb* our grief, like a junkie seeking a quick hit of whatever allows reprieve and quiets the voice of pain and loss even for a moment. We seek to piece together moment after moment of disconnection, sad to sober up and find that reality hasn't shifted, and the voice has only grown louder. Running from pain is the cultural norm because pain is seen as a nuisance. As Tim Keller says, "In the secular view, suffering is never seen as a meaningful part of life but only as an interruption."[3] We must push back against this temptation, again and again. The illusion that somehow all this running is the right way to cope feeds into the illusion of a life that doesn't exist. Maybe you've been there, maybe you are there, and maybe it's finally time to take a new approach.

UNHURRIED AND HONEST

Unhurried honesty has to be the place we start; it has to be the posture of our heart. This doesn't mean for a minute that we have it altogether and that our emotions aren't all over the place. If this were the case, you probably wouldn't have picked up this book. This also isn't a call to make your home here or to allow grief to become all-encompassing for all of life—not at all. But before we can become honest *in* the pain and loss (which we'll get to), we have to become honest *about* the pain and loss.

Here, let me state this as a question because I find that's often an easier way to ensure we're all on the same page and there's no confusion. No matter where you find yourself, no matter how worn out you might be, how apathetic, confused, angry, sad, anxious you might feel, and no matter how chaotic or out of order (a.k.a. life is a mess!) things might be, are you willing to slow down and be honest? Not perfectly put together, not completely ready to even receive, just honest, unhurried, and open?

Hopefully you said yes even if it was with hesitation. Believe me, I understand the hesitation. This approach took me years and many hours of therapy to be okay with. I went about it the hard and incredibly painful way, but my hope is that you'll take the better, less arduous route. Also, just to make it clear, this book isn't about me and it's not about my wife Laura. No, it's about all of us collectively. I really mean that. It's about not suffering in silence but walking together and surrounding one another with care, compassion, understanding, and truth, knowing that others are in a similar place but under the same God. It's taking a communal approach with a communal God who even in the most broken places (we'll get into this more later), I still believe is altogether good. Altogether understood? No. Altogether good? Yes.

INVISIBLE GRIEF DEFINED

Let me pause for a minute and fully define the kind of grief we're going to be talking about. As I shared in the introduction (go read it if you didn't!) grief is most commonly viewed through the lens of loss of life or loss of relationship (such as divorce). Invisible grief, the pain and loss of hopes, dreams, and good desires, is very different and yet very real.

What does invisible grief look like? It can take many forms. For example, it could be singleness for those who desire marriage; it could be infertility for those who desire children; it could be abandonment that prevents certain relationships; it could be a mental or physical chronic illness or disability that prevents you from pursuing certain aspects of life and community; or it could be a combination of these. It could be a series of circumstances that have brought you to a place you never expected to be and have kept you in a place you never wanted to stay.

There are two main markers that define invisible grief.

First, regardless of the intensity of the grief, it's often long term. It may stretch for a season or throughout all of life. For some, this grief may feel like a looming gray cloud that seems to envelope your day-to-day life. For others it may feel like a small stone in your shoe: it doesn't ruin your day, but you know it's there. Both are valid, and throughout different seasons we may vacillate between both feelings or experiences.

Second, there are no memories to attach to this kind of grief which means there is no love to cling to because there is no love lost. The old saying, "grief is love with nowhere to go," doesn't apply here. With invisible grief, there is pain and loss that doesn't have a place to go because of a future that doesn't, or hasn't yet come to exist. Sure, there may be a form of reality that we create in our minds, daydreams about what could have been, what could be, or what might be, but there are no actual memories to recall or cherish. This can become increasingly painful because there is no bottom floor. We can go as deep as our minds and hearts will allow, into the cavernous unknown of our most painful reality. Although grief in and of itself will carry some similar traits regardless of form, this is what makes this kind of grief unique, valid, and valuable. It may be more invisible in nature, but it's just as real and worthy of care.

In every chapter you're going to read real stories of real people with their own invisible grief, people that I have counseled, pastored, or met over the years. Because invisible grief can take on so many different forms, my hope is that these unique stories connect with you in profound and meaningful ways. That said, it would be unfair for me to ask you to be honest and not lead with honesty myself.

MEET DREW AND LAURA

My wife Laura and I (and from here on out we'll take off the "my wife" part) grew up in the same city and went to the same church. She'll want me to make it clear that she isn't *from* Missouri, but her family moved to Missouri when she was ten. She will always and forever claim that Tennessee is where she feels the closest to home. Yes, I was the eleven-year-old class clown, who talked way too much and sported an amazing bowl cut. Laura, on the other hand, was the more reserved ten-year-old with great manners, an irate ability to follow rules, and curly blond pigtails. We were in the same youth group and went on the same mission trips, and finally after my freshmen year of college I realized, "Hey, I should really get to know this girl more!" On our second date in the parking lot of the Stadium 12 Theater I may or may not have told her I loved her and was going to marry her (this is not recommended). Okay, I may have jumped the gun a little, but my nineteen-year-old feelings were strong and it turns out I was right! After graduating college with our respective degrees—hers in early childhood education, and mine in pastoral studies—we were married. With all of the hope and ambition two kids in their early twenties could muster, we moved to Atlanta and started our lives together.

Laura and I both grew up with siblings. Laura is the oldest of four and I was the youngest of three. Having a family in the future was a given for us. After five years filled with new adventures, new jobs, new cities, and new opportunities, we came to a crossroads moment. As I pursued a seminary degree I felt a major pull toward church-planting, especially in more unchurched cities. Soon an amazing opportunity presented itself and we put our house up for sale, packed up, said tearful goodbyes to family and friends on the east coast, and moved to the opposite end of the country. We were Seattle-bound and ready, or at least so we thought, for another adventure.

By this time I was twenty-eight years old and Laura just a year behind. We both felt a growing desire to have children and grow our family. We couldn't wait to have a house filled with toys scattered around, closets filled with baby clothes, bottles taking over the kitchen, and everything else that comes with the joy of new life. We were even excited about the late-night wake-ups. So we started trying and were sure it would only be a short matter of time before I came home from work one day and Laura would be waiting there with a positive pregnancy test tucked behind her back, a glowing smile on her face, and the two most magical words rolling off her tongue, "we're pregnant!" But month after month those words never came. Eventually we found ourselves in a doctor's office undergoing tests and then waiting for the results to try and see if there was any reason for the delay or if this was just a matter of patience.

The doctor started by sharing that all of Laura's results looked great. There was nothing preventing her from becoming pregnant at a biological level. Then the doctor turned to me. I can't remember much of what was said as numbers were shared and technical terms used, but I do remember the words "virtually impossible" coming out of her mouth and with every fiber of my being I remember the feeling of wanting to somehow someway push those words back in. As we processed this information—or at least tried to as best we could in a cold office that felt colder and more like a prison by the minute—our doctor shared that there was a procedure that might be able to fix what was happening. Without any hesitation we opted to move forward with the surgery and several weeks later I was on an operating room table at the University of Washington hospital only a few miles down the road from our house. Before I share any further, true confession time. As soon as I'm administered anesthesia or am coming off anesthesia I become everyone's best friend and incredibly emotional. As I lay on that bed I can vividly remember tearfully thanking anyone and everyone in the room for the service they were about to perform and what it meant to me. Apparently when I came off the anesthesia I was attempting to get out of the bed and hug all of the doctors, to Laura's embarrassment. I can see her eyes roll even as I write this.

After I was fully recovered, and with our hopes renewed, we started trying again. Once again, I found myself in the ever-optimistic state of wondering if today's the day I come home to hear those two amazing words. Instead, six months later we found ourselves back in the doctor's office for a follow-up that confirmed the surgery had not been successful. But there was still one more procedure that might lead to the results we were looking for. Just like before, there was no hesitation and weeks later it felt like deja-vu as we took the same drive to UW, put on the hospital gown, got hooked up to IVs, gave my tearful yet joyful hugs, and went under the knife. This time had to work. There was no way God would allow for this incredibly good desire to go unmet.

I was a pastor for goodness' sake, and Laura would be about as good a mother as it gets. I wouldn't even entertain the idea that this wouldn't work out like the end of every Disney movie I ever watched as a kid—with us all living happily ever after. Unfortunately, real life doesn't bend to the wonderfully naive structure of fairytales. This time we didn't have to wait to find out the results, as I was coming off the anesthesia the doctor came into the recovery room and shared with Laura that the surgery had been unsuccessful. I only have fuzzy memories of the moments that followed but I can still see Laura's eyes welling up with tears as reality hit. Outside of a miracle of God, she would never share—and I would never hear—those two magical and now distant, faint, painstaking words, "I'm pregnant."

We went home to the deafening silence of an empty home and I spent the next three days recovering in bed, putting on a brave face when Laura was in the room, even making light of the situation in failed attempts to somehow alleviate the pain I knew she was feeling, and then filling the pillow with tears as soon as the door would close. I sat in that bedroom on 15th avenue for three days, going back and forth between sadness, depression, anger, and shame. I felt like a complete failure, the thief who robbed my wife of the future we dreamed about, and less than a man. I was on an emotional roller-coaster, and at the same time, unwilling to acknowledge the full weight of this life-altering reality. Any time I would feel too much or start to think too deeply, I would flip an internal switch and, in essence, run from it. This is what I knew; this is what felt natural and safe. This wasn't a new practice for me.

We can refer to these as coping mechanisms, but in the case of grief the most fitting terminology might be "trauma behaviors." As Tiffany Sauber Millacci, Ph.D., shares in a recent article on this topic, these behaviors may look like *bad* behaviors but are instead what we call "trauma" or "survival behaviors" developed to deal with the stress, fear, tension, anxiety, or frustrations.[4] For as long as I could remember I would deal with pain either by minimizing, dismissing, or quickly covering it with humor and avoidance. We all have these tendencies or temptations. When the pain becomes too great, feels too hard to face, hits too close to home, or lasts for too long, we often put trauma behaviors into place. Why? We want relief; we're afraid of what might happen if we slow down and process the monster in the closet. These behaviors manifest in overeating, overspending, hyper-sexualization, pornography, cultivating busyness, or substance abuse to name a few. Anything that keeps us from having to sit next to the bomb that's been dropped into our lives.

I won't sugarcoat it: during the first few years of our new reality called infertility, I resorted to alcohol as a way to numb the pain because that's what I really wanted—to go numb. I bought into the cultural definition of dealing with pain, as summed up perfectly by musician Noah Kahn in his song "Growing Sideways": "Yeah, it's better to die numb than feel at all."[5] To me, it was easier than talking about it, thinking about, or working through it. Alcohol became a go-to and ever-present companion. It became a silent friend in the darkness that I knew wouldn't press or ask questions. I'm feeling too much, take a drink. I'm too anxious, take a drink. Another panic attack, take a drink. It would take three years before I would be forced to face the pain and loss of what would never be and see it for what it really was. Whether you can relate or you're in a healthy place and just need to be affirmed, the good news is we don't have to keep running. There really is a better way.

SLOWING DOWN TO LAMENT

I don't know if you've read Lamentations lately but I'd bet the answer is no. It's one of the most avoided books in the Bible. It's not a best-seller for sermon series and you won't find commentaries on the book jumping off the shelf. If you aren't familiar, Lamentations involves a man (most likely Jeremiah) sitting with, contemplating, and puzzling over the results of evil and suffering in the world. God's people have been hit by tragedy and a desired future is now non-existent.

> How lonely sits the city
> that was full of people!
> How like a widow has she become,
> she who was great among the nations!
> She who was a princess among the provinces
> has become a slave.
>
> *She weeps bitterly in the night,*
> *with tears on her cheeks;*
> *among all her lovers*
> *she has none to comfort her;*
> *all her friends have dealt treacherously with her;*
> *they have become her enemies.* (Lam. 1:1-2, emphasis mine)

It's important and fitting that the writer laments what has happened and the ripple effect this has on the future. To lament, meaning to show passionate grief and sorrow over a major loss, is right and healthy and yet it's completely uncomfortable and foreign to our western way of living. We are going to look at the process and necessity of lament in much greater detail later in the book, but for now let's simply recognize that it has become a foreign concept for many. We are a people who have lost the art and discipline of lamenting for the sake of avoiding pain at all cost and giving in to the pressure of society's rules surrounding grief.

THE PAIN AND THE PRESSURE

In the words of one of my favorite bands, Jimmy Eat World, "It takes my pain away!"[6] We are desperate to rid ourselves of even the slightest pain and will often go to great lengths to make sure that happens. It makes sense: who wants to sit with pain? No one in their right mind willingly desires to be in pain, invites pain into their lives, or asks it to stay for just a little longer. We aren't modern day masochists. To state it frankly, if pain is bad, how can slowing down and sitting with it be good? This is incredibly paradoxical and yet unbelievably important when it comes to your grief. In the pain and the pressure we find both an internal and external force. The pain produced from the inside, combined with pressure from the outside, result in a powerful impulse to run.

If we don't learn to first sit with the pain, we will inevitably wear ourselves out. We'll go up and down the hills, passing it by, circling around it, in the process taking on anxiety, frustration, resentment, and apathy. Not to mention our view of God distorts as our unattended wound festers and grows in size. While God has no desire to see this happen, this is one of Satan's favorite playgrounds. If he can keep you running, he can keep you from the truth your broken heart longs for. If he can keep you searching out in the cold, working as hard as you can to fix the problem on your own, he can keep you from the warm embrace of a heavenly Father who has sat with His own pain and loss and who is intimately aquainted with yours.

Yes, we've been taught that pain is bad, and so we avoid it where we can. It is true that pain was never a part of our creator's original, perfect plan, and yet, at the same time, as C.S Lewis so eloquently puts it in his book, *The Problem of Pain,* "God whispers to us in our pleasures, speaks in our consciences, but shouts in our pain."[7] I will say this multiple times throughout the book in hopes that it sinks into your soul as much as I've needed it to sink into mine over the years as it's served as a healing balm in my darkest nights and brightest days. With God nothing is wasted. We often cause ourselves so much more suffering by avoiding reality, instead of accepting what actually is.

This reminds me of the bison. I remember reading something years ago about these mammoth animals. During the most intense winter storms, unlike every other animal, they are known to turn and face the storm. In the howling winds and sideways snow, these animals know that heading into the storm, and facing what is, will help shorten the length of their time in the storm as they live out in vast open spaces.

It is impossible to heal from what we're not willing to face. We are only delaying, and in turn bottling up, more and more pain and suffering that God wants to actually hold *with* us as He cares *for* us.

As if pain weren't enough, we also have pressure that serves as the other side of the coin. This pressure takes many forms and—like the last kid standing on the losing team in dodgeball waiting for the other team to hurl each ball they can find—it comes at us from everywhere. Now pressure may seem disconnected to grief but I promise you it's not. Think about the culture we live in. We are hurried to the point that busyness is worn like a badge of honor, when in actuality, it's more like a hospital bracelet. We are spoon-fed the idea that faster is better: it's more advantageous, a sign of success, and should be applied to every aspect of our lives. We ditch meaningful conversations for hurried hellos and goodbyes and displace priorities for the sake of productivity. When we take this ideology and apply it to a real person experiencing real, long-term grief, it's inevitable we'll feel the pressure to move on, to get past it, to not make others feel uncomfortable or take too much of their time. This type of pressure can be quick to produce a suppression of suffering and, often unintentionally, a dishonest life. Because we feel this cultural and personal pressure, we put on a smile and we act like all is well, even though we know nothing could be further from the truth.

We are not a people who stop to lament; we are not a people who stop to admit that life has gone off the road and we don't have the ability to pull ourselves out of the ditch. We are a people to pull ourselves up by our bootstraps and keep going. We don't sit with pain, we push through it. We don't stop to examine the rubble, we rebuild. We don't admit defeat or weakness—a loser's lot—no, we are more. We are better than that. We are fully capable, in control, and a formidable force for whatever threatens what we've worked so hard to cultivate. If there's a problem, we'll solve it. If there's a roadblock, we'll remove it. We are a people who move ahead and leave the past in the dust.

Here's the problem: invisible grief doesn't play by this set of rules or arrogant notions. Invisible grief doesn't care about your fairy-tale delusions, and it's not here to barter. Invisible grief in its true form is often, long-haul grief: it may vary in its degree of severity, from person to person or season to season, but it will be a part of our lives, either for an extended season or permanently. So we have a choice: will we run, or will we stop and allow honesty to come out of hiding?

This reminds me of Jesus' words to the man at Bethesda in the Gospel of John, chapter 5. We know that this man was an invalid for thirty-eight years. He was completely reliant on others to move him from one place to the other. We also know by his own words that he felt completely defeated and stuck because of his circumstances. Jesus approached and asked this question, "Do you want to be healed?" (v. 6). Allow Him in this moment to ask you the same: Do you want to get well? Do you want to heal, or do you prefer to stay where you are? While the answer may seem obvious, never underestimate the feeling of comfort and safety that encourages us to stay in our brokenness, especially if we've been there for a long season. Like this man, we can become too familiar with our circumstantial reality and have trouble seeing any aspect of potential healing in front of us. There is the unknown. What if I do face this? What if I do offer this up? What's on the other side?

"Do you want to be healed?"

If we want to get well we have to start by allowing honesty to make its way into the living room of our disheveled hearts and bring grace along as a welcomed guest. I love Brennan Manning's take on this:

> When I get honest, I admit I am a bundle of paradoxes. I believe and I doubt, I hope and get discouraged, I love and I hate, I feel bad about feeling good, I feel guilty about not feeling guilty. I am trusting and suspicious. I am honest and I still play games. Aristotle said I am a rational animal; I say I am an angel with an incredible capacity for beer.

> To live by grace means to acknowledge my whole life story, the light side and the dark. In admitting my shadow side I learn who I am and what God's grace means.[8]

SAFE AND SECURE

Safe, seen, soothed, and secure. We all long for this kind of secure attachment. This starts in our earliest years, but the hunger continues throughout life. This theory was developed by Dr. Dan Siegel, clinical professor of psychiatry at UCLA. Security is something often focused on when studying infants and parenting but it is an ongoing need for all of us.[9]

These four needs for secure attachment, I would argue, are a necessity when it comes to the intersection of our relationship with God, our grief, and the ability to stop running. It's only when we believe that, through Christ, we are safe with, seen by, soothed by, and secure with God, that we feel comfortable enough to walk through our invisible grief with honest, unhurried vulnerability.

Imagine being out in a storm. You went for a routine walk in the woods and out of nowhere the rain starts to pour and won't let up. You are cold, soaked, have several open cuts from falling along the way, and are completely worn out. You see a beautiful home ahead with lights on the porch. You approach. Now think of the four "S's" as you get to the beautifully ornate door with a giant lock preventing you from entering the home—a home with a kind host, a crackling fire, food to nourish you, and a warm blanket. What opens this door? Grace. Grace is the key. The untamed, unmatched, unearned, and undeserved grace of Jesus allows us to come in from the storm. Grace that allows us to admit that we walk with a limp, that we are in fact ragamuffins in need of good news. This same grace allows us to sit, to listen, and to heal. It reminds us we are not alone and we never will be. It's the grace of Jesus that offers the invitation, "Take my yoke upon you, and learn from me, for I am gentle and lowly in heart, and you will find rest for your souls. For my yoke is easy, and my burden is light" (Matt. 11:29-30).

"God loves you just the way you are, but He refuses to leave you that way."[10] It's time to stop running in the woods and come in from the storm. In all of our pain, in all of our loss, in all of the unknown, grace is the well from which we must draw and drink as it reminds us that we are indeed safe, seen, soothed, and secure in Christ. All of these things are true between God and His children.

As a reminder of this, before we move any further, I want you to take a moment and let these words, inspired by Psalm 23 and read in the second person, wash over you and give you permission not to run, but to rest. Read them a few times, let them sink in.

The Lord is your shepherd; You shall not want.

He makes you lie down in green pastures.
He leads you beside still waters.

He restores your soul.
He leads you in paths of righteousness for His name's sake.

Even though you walk through the valley of the shadow of death, you will fear no evil, for He is with you; His rod and His staff, they comfort you.

He prepares a table before you in the presence of your enemies.

He anoints your head with oil; your cup overflows.

Surely goodness and mercy shall follow you all the days of your life, and you shall dwell in the house of the Lord forever.

REFLECTIONS

1. What is your invisible grief? How long has it been present in your life?

2. If you feel, or have felt, the temptation to run from the grief, has it been to run from, through, or around it? What's at the core of this temptation for you?

3. Is there any fear associated with taking an unhurried, honest approach and facing your grief? If so, what is the fear? What does grace have to say in the face of this fear?

THE LIES WE BELIEVE

I remember my grandfather telling me the story of Orson Welles' infamous *Mercury Theatre* radio show from 1938. If you're not familiar, on October 30, 1938, as a Halloween episode, Orson Welles directed and narrated an adaptation of H.G. Wells' novel *The War of the Worlds* live on the radio in prime-time over the CBS radio network.[1] Much like the television today, the radio was a centerpiece in most homes. Families would gather around and listen to music specials, stand-up comedy routines, and narrated stories that would stir the imagination of listeners young and old, a true picture of the wonderful Americana landscape of the past (alright, I'm getting off track). Orson Welles was an incredibly gifted writer, director, actor, and even magician (co-writing and starring in arguably the greatest film of all time, *Citizen Kane*). On this particular evening, he was a little too good, and he incited a panic among many listeners who became convinced that an actual Martian invasion was taking place! With the radio station intentionally forgoing commercial interruption, listeners took in this news-bulletin format and began to prepare for the worst. In hindsight this is, well, hilarious, but at the time Orson Welles would have to spend the next day explaining to reporters that he never intended to cause a panic and apologizing to listeners who'd believed this fictitious production and had acted accordingly. It's amazing what our minds can capture as truth, even when the foundation of truth is completely lacking. What we believe has a dramatic effect on how we live.

We live in a time where lies and misinformation spread like wildfire across our television screens, social media, and society. It can be incredibly difficult to know who to trust and what to believe. We long for honesty and at the same time are fearful that it might be too much for our heads and hearts to handle, especially when it hits close to home. The longer invisible grief, and the new reality it carries, persists the easier it is for lies to creep into our minds and make their way to our hearts. We may cognitively *know* what's true or reasonable, and yet it's functionality that ultimately matters. It's one thing to know that something isn't your fault and it's another thing for you to functionally live that out. This is the troublesome tension between our head and our heart, where in between we find truth and lies butted up against one another fighting for control. This is a prevalent problem with invisible grief and is due to the length of time we sit with the pain and loss of what has never been and may never be. What does this mean? Well, it means that we need to not only be on guard against the real and present danger of lies taking root, but we also need to reinforce the truth every step of the way like mini sandbags stacked against the shore as a storm prepares to make landfall. Think of these lies that can make their way into our lives, sitting beneath our grief like bombs waiting to go off and destroy all truth in sight. In essence we must be in the practice of dismantling the bombs and rendering helpless the lies we are tempted to believe, lies that seek to destroy and distract us from the truth God so desperately wants us to cling to.

ILLUSORY CORRELATION

Our mind is an amazing organ filled with complexity and wonder. With over 86 billion neurons, 2.5 million gigabytes of storage, and over 50,000 thoughts per day, the human brain is truly magnificent. With neurons traveling at a speed of 150 mph and generating enough electricity to power a low voltage light bulb (12–25 watts!), our brains are a finely tuned, mysterious, intricately designed gift from God.[2] At the same time, our brains are not immune to false beliefs. Lies may start small, but they can become overwhelming. I don't know if you're familiar with the term illusory correlation, but understanding this concept can be incredibly helpful to understanding why we believe what we believe, even if it couldn't be further from the truth. Essentially, illusory correlation is when we see an association between two variables (events, actions, ideas, etc.) when they aren't actually associated.[3] When we apply this to invisible grief this looks like the connection we make between the pain and loss we are experiencing and a perceived cause behind it or false idea we've bought into. "I want to be married, but I'm not married yet. If I just had more faith in God He would give me a spouse." "We want to have children, we can't have children. This must be God punishing us for past sin." There are many lies surrounding our grief that we can start to believe. Instead of avoidance, let's stare them down and take some time to expose and dismantle some of the most prevalent lies.

FOUR LIES

1. Bad Things Don't Happen to Good Christians

In western Christianity there's a growing epidemic and hunger for the gospel of prosperity. It's bought and sold in the marketplace every day and is all over social media. Celebrity pastors, Christian life coaches and the like, all attempting to serve up a more palatable version of Christianity where faith in God results in an abundant life of wealth, health, and immeasurable success. This prosperity gospel finds its birth in the Healing Revivals of the 1950s where the atonement was falsely interpreted as to include the alleviation of sickness and poverty, viewed as curses to be broken by faith.[4] Fast forward thirty years and televangelists found that this was a great way to not only gain viewership, but amass a small (or not so small) fortune by preying on desperate individuals who would send in money for the promise of healing, wealth, or escape from hardship. I get it, who doesn't like the idea of a God who gives us everything we've ever wanted and keeps us from experiencing pain? Here's one of many problems with this ideology: it's predicated on the amount of faith you can muster and bleeds into a secondary lie of, "if you just have more faith, ____." If you just have more faith, God will give you that child. If you just have enough faith, God will give you that spouse. If you just have enough faith, God will heal you. Or even worse, if you'd just *had* more faith, God wouldn't have taken your son. If you'd just *had* more faith, God would have healed your child. The dangers of such a manipulated gospel are never-ending and often result in fear, shame, and doubt when the bottom drops out…and in life, it's inevitable that at times, the bottom will drop out. As one of my professors once told me, "a gospel that can't be shared to the most impoverished person, in the most impoverished third-world country, shouldn't be shared in ours." When real life hits, when real pain and loss become present, a prosperity-driven gospel can only mean two things: Either I've failed God, or God has failed me. This gospel completely negates the reality of living in a broken world, with broken bodies, resulting in broken dreams. This isn't a loving gospel, it's a selfish, man-made monster of the cruelest kind, one that opens the door to cold, apathetic lies instead of the empathetic truth our hearts need to hear.

There are two distinct promises God gives to His children: Life *will* be hard, but I *will* be with you. Jesus Himself makes this clear in John 16:33 when He says, "In the world you will have tribulation. But take heart; I have overcome the world." When we take a close look at Scripture we see account after account of people who love Jesus facing incredible pain and loss. While simply knowing this isn't enough, it starts to redirect us toward what's actually true. As I've thought about this lie—that when piercing our conscience can fester and lead us to doubt, anger, even resentment toward God—I often turn to the life of David, literally a man after God's own heart (1 Sam. 13:14). Specifically, it takes me to a part of David's young life where he's been so incredibly faithful in following God, where his faith is unmatched and his humility unheard of. And yet, this man of God faces incredible hardship. On paper it doesn't make sense. He's done everything God has asked, and all of a sudden he's running for his life and hiding out in caves with a band of misfits. In Psalm 34, as he sits in one of these caves, David pens the words, "Many are the afflictions of the righteous…" Unfortunately my friend, none of us is immune to difficulty, and this doesn't have anything to do with being a good Christian or having enough faith. How do we combat this lie? We finish the second half of Psalm 34:19 and cling to this truth with a heavenly perspective. "Many are the afflictions of the righteous…but the Lord delivers him out of them all." (More on that to come.)

2. I'm Being Punished

This lie hits home more than any other on a personal level. It paralyzed me time and time again and took me back to past sins and failures that God in His grace had already freed me from. Like a prison inmate released without any conditions,

I would find myself lowering my head, taking the long walk down the dark hall, and willingly sitting back down in the cold cell I had already been freed from. The cell door was always open, I was always free to leave, but sometimes the lie felt too heavy for me to pick up my feet and walk out the other side. I would sit alone in the darkness with only one object in the room with me, a projector filled with slides of my past. I would play them on repeat. With every click, shame and condemnation flooded in, the waves crashing over my head and pulling me further and further away from the shore of truth.

This isn't a new lie. We're going to look at this encounter on a deeper level a bit later, but let's take a look at John 9 for a minute as Jesus encounters, and subsequently heals, a man born blind. Jesus' own disciples' first assumption isn't that this man was born blind because Adam and Eve sinned in the garden, it's that God is clearly punishing this man. "As he passed by, he saw a man blind from birth. And his disciples asked him, 'Rabbi, who sinned, this man or his parents, that he was born blind?'" (vv. 1-2). I love Jesus' answer to the disciples who, like us, can become easily confused. "Jesus answered, 'It was not that this man sinned, or his parents, but that the works of God might be displayed in him.'" (v. 3). Wow! Not only does Jesus cut the head off of this untruth, He affirms that even in this man's affliction there's purpose, not pointless pain, and definitely not punishment.

This lie, born in the deep wells of the past, is one of the most prevalent for those walking through invisible grief because we know ourselves all too well. We know we aren't perfect, far from it! This is perhaps one of the easiest lies to apply to our circumstances because it makes the most sense. I've come to believe it's often far easier for us to understand the depth of our sins, than the depth of God's grace. One feels too true and the other feels too good to be true, and so we default to punishment. I mean technically it's true that because of our sin we aren't deserving of any good thing, but to believe that the painful circumstance or reality in our life is God's punishment completely negates and rips out the heart of the gospel. I don't want to sound too intense here, but this lie pulls Jesus off the cross, backfills the grave, and erases the three days in between from human history. Let me say this as clearly as I can for myself and for you: God is not punishing His children. He has no punishment left, it was completely poured out on Jesus. Only grace remains! Does God discipline His beloved kids, yes, but always for our good, always for restoration of the relationship. Punishment has been put to death once and for all.

In the relentless love of Christ, every burden of your past and future has been lifted, completely paid for by His grace. You're no longer a prisoner to guilt or regret; you're free. You don't need to lash yourself with the chains of shame, nor do you need to return to the empty prisons of your own making. In His arms there is mercy and there is forgiveness, and there lies the truth that you are wholly embraced. I want you to write your name in this blank. Seriously, grab a pencil, pen, marker, or crayon, and write your name down. _____, your grief is not God's punishment. God has a lot of things for you—love, patience, kindness, compassion, mercy— but punishment is not one of them. I want so badly to sit with you right now, to look into your eyes, and speak these words to you face-to-face. These are words I needed to hear in my darkest hours and words I still need to hear today. I love Eugene Peterson's paraphrase of Isaiah 43:25. I pray this washes over you, and for those who need it, begins to gently erase the lie that punishment is the reason for your ongoing grief. "But I, yes I (God), am the One who takes care of your sins—that's what I do. I don't keep a list of your sins."[5]

3. Time Heals All Wounds.

To find the source of this amazing bit of advice we have to go all the way back to 300 B.C. and the Greek poet Menander.[6] I get the sentiment, I think we all do. There's this idea that if we simply give it time, the grief will grow smaller and smaller until it just disappears. If only that were true. If only we had to just sit back, kick our feet up, and wait for all of the pain and loss to exit our hearts and minds.

MEET AARON

I want to introduce you to my friend Aaron. I've known Aaron for the past five years. We've co-led Bible studies together, he's been a strong leader within our men's ministry at ONE Fellowship, and his beautiful family are core members of the church. From the outside, you would probably assume Aaron had a normal, healthy upbringing, but that isn't the case.

Aaron was born into a single parent household back in the 1970s. The term single parent would even be a stretch as he was passed around to different family members.

> To not have both parents wasn't fashionable at this time and I can vividly remember the absence of a dad from a very young age. I remember filling out forms in school where you had to share things about your mother and your father and there was a void of my father and I would be asked, "Who's your dad?"

At a very young age, Aaron was told his dad was a famous photographer and was given a name but that was the extent of it.

Throughout Aaron's adolescent years, he would have father figures who would come in and out of his life. One of these was his uncle Dennis who he lived with for a time. Unfortunately, on his way home one night, his uncle died in a motorcycle accident. Aaron was old enough to start connecting these dots and the loss of his uncle wrecked him. Not only was his biological father not in his life, now the one man who resembled a father was gone.

To ensure you understand the hand Aaron was dealt, his mother had almost aborted him but, in the end, had decided to keep him. In Aaron's own words, "Whatever she did in not abandoning me pre-birth she definitely made up for after I was born." From birth to fifth grade Aaron was passed around to different family members. He and his mother were both physically and emotionally separated. Aaron was a little kid being told that his mom didn't want anything to do with him; all the while his mom was calling him but was never allowed to talk with Aaron. While family members thought they were doing right by Aaron, they were creating deep wounds that wouldn't manifest for many years to come. Even many of those who took Aaron in were not stable themselves. He found himself in physically and emotionally abusive environments at a very young age.

In the fifth grade Aaron was reunited with his mother and stayed with her from that time forward, but this wasn't a happily-ever-after situation. His mother was very poor and had very little to offer. Aaron recalls trips to empty bar parking lots early on Saturday mornings. He and his mother would collect any money that was accidentally discarded by intoxicated patrons. They would then take that money, however much or little, and have breakfast.

When Aaron hit college, his mother wanted him to connect with his biological father. It didn't really matter to Aaron, or so he told himself. As he went along with his mother's plans it would turn out that who his mother believed to be his father all of these years was, in fact, not. All of a sudden it did matter, and it felt like another unexpected wound was opened.

As Aaron grew older, he developed a plug-in response when people would ask about his father. By uttering the phrase "I don't have contact with him," most people wouldn't press any further. Eventually, by his thirties, Aaron was so desperate to avoid thinking about it that he became comfortable believing that he didn't need to know who he was. "I either did my best to avoid this altogether or had a quick answer so I could move on."

Five years ago, Aaron signed up for ancestry.com. His curiosity took hold, and he started down the path of trying to piece together more of his origin story. One weekend Aaron was leaving for a trip, but he asked his wife Lindsey to look at something that popped up. When he arrived back home Lindsey gently approached and said, "we need to talk." Through the research there was a hit on Aaron's paternal side of the family. In talking with his mother and by connecting more dots, it was confirmed that they had located his biological father. The mystery was solved, but the man who Aaron never met, the man who left a mark by leaving no mark at all, had passed away. There would be no reunion, no opportunity for questions, no sense of relational connection. This was another hard hit among many, but at least there was an answer.

For Aaron this wouldn't be the end of the story. Although time had passed and everything in him wanted to move on, that's just not how invisible grief works. Aaron and Lindsey have two children, Rowen and Brooke. One day, without any warning and decades having passed, grief walked through the door. Aaron was sitting in his living room. His son Rowen walked into the room, about eleven years old at the time. The light caught Aaron's son. Aaron could see himself in Rowen, the child he loved, and suddenly a flood of emotions hit him. Anger. Feelings of abandonment. "I would never do that to my son, how could she do that to me?"

Time didn't heal the wounds; it just provided an opportunity to suppress them. "Until Rowen walked into the room I didn't know that grief was there. Like a backpack, I just pushed it down and thought I could just move on and live life." Thankfully Aaron took this realization as an opportunity, not a burden. Soon after, he would find himself on a men's hike that would be transformative and allow for newfound peace among the ashes of what never was with his mother and would never be with his father. At one point on the hike Aaron was asked a question, "who do you need to forgive?" As he sat and prayed, the Holy Spirit made it abundantly clear: "you need to ask your mom for forgiveness." "Woah," Aaron thought, "I think you got that wrong. Who do we need to forgive, not who needs my forgiveness." The Holy Spirit's prompting was further confirmed through a rock ceremony where men would put a word on a rock—something they needed to leave on the mountain—and then they would pick up a word to take with them. Aaron wrote "abandonment" and threw it into the water. What he picked up was "adopted son."

Aaron knew that as soon as he got home he needed to meet with his mom. With his pastor by his side, all three sat in his backyard. There was a surreal moment of peace and quiet in Aaron's backyard, as a yard close to a street that is normally filled with noise became beautifully silent. "When I asked for her to forgive me, the Holy Spirit allowed me to see her differently. She didn't understand why, she knew she should be the one apologizing. As we broke down so did the wall between us." Aaron's mother would pass eighteen months later but for those eighteen months there would be a drastic shift in the relationship. Where there once was only pain, forgiveness and reconciliation would make its way through. Anytime his mother would come into the room, he was able to see her in a completely different light. God had begun to restore what time never could.

* * *

"Time heals all wounds." This statement, which has been adopted and passed on by well-meaning friends, family, and acquaintances is not only untrue when it comes to grief in general, but it also flies in the face of the type of chronic grief we're talking about here. It also goes a step further and puts an imaginary timer on the grief we experience, as if that's how real life works. "Okay kid, you have two weeks and three days to sit with your grief and then it's time to let it go." We touched on this in the last chapter but one of the reasons we offer up this idea, or even believe it ourselves, is often twofold. We are either uncomfortable or unwilling to walk alongside those experiencing ongoing grief for the long haul, or we are uncomfortable or unwilling to truly acknowledge the multi-faceted nature of our own grief, and so we choose the passive route of waiting and hoping for it to pass. I was recently listening to the new album from one of my favorite singer-songwriters out of the U.K., Benjamin Francis Leftwich entitled *Some Things Break* and his lyrics resonated with me as they touch on this very idea. "If time is a healer, how long will it be, before I recover, before I can feel? Love for the bruised and the broken in me. If time is a healer, it's patient with me."[7]

If you get to know me you'll soon come to find that I have a growing collection of shoes, enjoy cooking and throwing parties, and love documentaries. There are countless classic movies I haven't seen that friends and family give me a hard time about, but chances are I can tell you all about an obscure documentary you just have to see! To that end, I've always been fascinated with the Kennedy family. I've watched several documentaries on the life of John F. and Bobby, and a few years ago watched a fantastic docu-series called *American Dynasty: The Kennedys*. Each episode took an in-depth look at the entire family. Theirs is by most accounts one of the most grief-stricken and tragedy-filled political families of recent history. Through all of the pain and all of the loss, the matriarch Rose Kennedy once spoke to the grief she and her family had endured. In a famous line she said, "It has been said, 'time heals all wounds.' I do not agree. The wounds remain. In time, the mind, protecting its sanity, covers them with scar tissue and the pain lessens. But it is never gone."[8] These are not the words of a philosopher, a poet, or a physiologist; these are the words of a mother who lost her sons, husband, and grandchildren. These are the words of someone who understands the power of grief at a visceral level. I believe Mrs. Kennedy is right that the wounds remain and that the pain is never gone, but for those who place their trust in Christ, there's so much more. Yes, at times our mind does seek to protect our sanity in a number of different ways, but what we really need is the careful hand of a heart surgeon, who, with precision, puts things back together, although differently and not without scars. More than that, we don't just need mental protection over time. We need a physician who can heal not just physically, but also spiritually and emotionally.

Out of all the healings of Jesus we find recorded in the Bible, I think the one that resonates with me the most is the healing of the demon-possessed man found in Mark 5. To sum up this account (go check it out in full later), Jesus and

His disciples arrive on the shore of a lake and are immediately met by a man who has been overtaken by a demonic force. "They came to the other side of the sea, to the country of the Gerasenes. And when Jesus had stepped out of the boat, immediately there met him out of the tombs a man with an unclean spirit. He lived among the tombs. And no one could bind him anymore, not even with a chain" (Mark 5:1-3). We soon learn that this man, once completely sane, has been taken over both physically and mentally to the point that the townspeople couldn't even contain him with chains. He spends his nights howling like an animal and has become such a danger that he's taken to live out his days among the dead in a graveyard. As Jesus shows His authority and forces the demons to leave the man and, upon their request, enter the bodies of pigs (seriously, you have to go read Mark 5 later), the farmers who are scared out of their minds run back to town to tell about what they've just seen.

As the townspeople come out, they find the man "sitting there, clothed and in his right mind" (v. 15). As Jesus goes to leave and get back in the boat, the man begs Jesus to take him with Him. You can imagine this emotional scene. Jesus redirects the man to instead be a missionary to his family and friends, to tell them about the amazing grace he has been shown by the great physician. Why do I love this healing so much? It shows Jesus' holistic healing power. It's clear that He has healed this man both physically, emotionally, and spiritually. Time can't do this, but Jesus can. The healing might take a different form than we expect and yes, pain in some form may remain, but in His goodness and kindness Jesus is able and willing to heal us. We'll take a deeper dive into this in a few chapters.

4. The Fallacy of Relative Privation

The fallacy of what? I know, let me explain. If you aren't familiar with the terminology, you'll definitely be familiar with the idea. This is when we dismiss problems by presenting bigger problems. Although I really don't like the terminology, this is often referred to as the "children are starving in Africa argument."[9] Essentially, anything less than the larger problem presented isn't that big of a deal or maybe isn't even worth recognition. This distorted idea seeks to wrap us in guilt and shame for acknowledging our own (very real) grief because there is inevitably someone whose grief we deem greater. With this lie we end up feeling bad about feeling bad and can move to suppress our grief.

I remember sitting in our living room and watching the news one night several years ago. We were in the throes of infertility but were also trying to steward our pain and loss well. A story came on covering a recent bombing in a Middle East town. The pictures that came across the screen were heartbreaking as mothers carried the bodies of their small children out of the rubble. I remember immediately feeling guilty that I felt bad about our circumstance in light of what this community was facing. Here's the question we have to answer: does someone else's pain make ours less real or relevant? Here's a follow up: does it do any good to suppress our own pain because greater pain (on paper) exists? The answer to both is a resounding, no! Should we feel empathy, compassion, sadness, pray for, and seek mercy for those who are hurting? Of course—and still we don't have to trade one pain for another. Your grief is just as important to God as anyone else's. You will not find a single verse in the Bible that asks us to take our pain and bury it because it's really not that bad in comparison. Quite the opposite, Jesus invites us to bring all of our burdens, every single one, to Him, "casting all your anxieties on him, because he cares for you"

(1 Pet. 5:7). There's that beautiful word again: care. And when *care* is combined with *all* we get a powerful picture of a loving Father who wants to sit with His kids and hear about every pain they face: the skinned knee, the paper cut, the broken arm, all of it. It all matters to Him.

THE GREATEST LIE

We could spend an entire book on the lies that attempt to infiltrate our lives. Undoubtedly there are many more than the four mentioned above. My hope is that even more than resonating with the lie itself, you resonate with the singular truth that combats it. Although life is hard, we have a God who is near, who loves us, and who cares deeply about every single part of us. Because this is true, even in the pain, even through the loss, we can still cling to something more real than the strongest lie. We can cling to a greater hope.

> We boast in the hope of the glory of God. And not only that, but we also boast in our afflictions, because we know that affliction produces endurance, endurance produces proven character, and proven character produces hope. This hope will not disappoint us, because God's love has been poured out in our hearts through the Holy Spirit who was given to us. (Rom. 5:2b-5, CSB)

Pushing back against the lies is an ongoing practice. Some days will be easier than others, and some days will be incredibly hard. We must give ourselves grace knowing that Jesus gives us more.

Now there's one more lie that we haven't covered here. It's the greatest and carries the most weight. It's so big it gets an entire chapter. It finds itself front and center in the tension of goodness and brokenness, and puts God on trial. It's a lie born in the garden of Eden, a lie that stretches into the here and now: Does God really care?

REFLECTIONS

1. Are there certain lies you have been believing about your grief? Jot them down.

2. How do lies (whether mentioned in this chapter or another) present as a roadblock to healing?

3. In response to the lie you may be wrestling with or have wrestled with, what would the gospel of Jesus have to say about that lie?

DOES GOD REALLY CARE?

MEET NICK

I met Nick in 2012 when I was a pastor at a church in Orange County, California. The church was hosting a large conference. I was assigned the role of hosting one of the speakers for the weekend. It just so happened this speaker would be Nick Vujicic. If you aren't familiar with Nick, his story is one of grief, grace, resolve, and inspiration on a level rarely seen. Nick was born in Melbourne, Australia in 1982 with a rare disorder called tetra-amelia syndrome. Nick's body was unable to form arms or legs. When Nick was born his mother and father were caught completely off guard and struggled to cope with their son's disorder. Nick has shared as part of his story how apologetic the doctors were to his parents for not identifying the disorder early enough to offer them the option of abortion. It was clear that life would not be easy for Nick.

> Looking at my brother and sister born after me—and them having arms and legs—kind of felt a little unfair and weird. And with no answers, it's easy to start believing

the lies, the little voices that say, "you're not good enough, you're a mistake, there is no greater purpose for your life," and so as I went to school, I was facing bullying. I went through depression at age eight until age twelve, and I felt like there was no hope for my life.[1]

At this tender age, one thing felt clear to Nick: God didn't care. "I convinced myself that there was no God. But if there was a God, He was simply unfair. I prayed for a miracle. And a miracle did not come."

At the age of ten, Nick didn't see how he could live a normal life and, feeling he was a burden to his family, attempted suicide by drowning himself in a bathtub. Thankfully, he was unsuccessful. I remember sitting in a greenroom with Nick as he shared this part of his story. I was absolutely speechless. To imagine a child this young carrying so much darkness and despair was unfathomable to me. Nick recounted how he came to the realization that his absence would be more of a burden on his family than his presence, and with that realization a newfound purpose started to take root.

Although Nick didn't have arms or legs, he did have a deformed foot. This would serve as remarkable motivation for Nick to move around with incredible balance and coordination. It was around the age of thirteen that he read the story of the blind man from John 9, and this had a profound impact on his life. He came to the astute realization that, "If God has a plan for the blind man, He has a plan for me." Of course, Nick was right. Not only did God draw close, but He also started to rearrange Nick's entire view on God's care.

Nick has an incredible passion for seeing people encounter Jesus and trust in Jesus, even through the grief and pain that life may bring. I recently listened to Nick on a podcast where he shared these incredible words of encouragement.

Here I am now at age forty, with a beautiful wife, four beautiful children, and this incredible ministry Life Without Limbs—being the hands and feet of God (even without hands and feet), standing in front of the gates of hell and redirecting traffic. I now try to encourage everyone that no matter what pain we go through, that God can do beautiful things with our broken pieces … if we give those broken pieces into His hands.

Nick refused to allow his broken pieces to become his identity; instead, he has allowed God to use his story and his love of Jesus to impact millions. Nick speaks all over the world, dozens of times a year to different audiences in different spaces, but always with the same message: there is grace and hope rooted in the person and work of Jesus.

MORE THAN A FEELING, MORE THAN A MOVE

We're going to tap into feelings and emotions more in a few chapters, but I would be remiss if I didn't bring it up here. Our feelings are absolutely valid and, at the same time, can lead us astray. I don't think this is a mind-blowing concept but it does help to voice it. I can't tell you how many conversations Laura and I had in our Seattle home where all of the filters were removed and we would stare at each other, completely worn out, and utter the words, "does God even care?" How could two thirty-something Christians, one who is actively pastoring a church, both who started a relationship with Jesus before they even learned how to swim, question God's care? Because it didn't *feel* like God cared. It felt like He was either choosing to go silent or had left the room and slammed the door on His way out. Again, we'll unpack more of this holistically in a few chapters, but this is a predominant lie entangled in chronic grief. It's a lie that we tend to wrestle with. It's also a lie that can be incredibly scary because it makes us question the very nature of our relationship with God. This question finds its origin story in Eden.

As Satan takes the form of a snake, with every intention of hurting God by deceiving those created in His very image, he whispers one question and one lie into Eve's ear and opens the door to a far greater doubt. "Did God actually say, 'You shall not eat of any tree in the garden'?" (Gen. 3:1). After Eve answers, Satan assures her that she will not surely die but will instead have her eyes opened and become like God, there and then asking, "Is God holding out on me? Does He really care?" Over the last two decades of pastoring, this question of care has come up time and time again as I've walked with people through their own grief. Care is a big deal. We have an innate desire to be cared for. As Rick Hanson, Ph.D. and senior fellow of the Greater Good Center at UC Berkeley, shares, "Studies show that feeling cared about buffers against stress, increases positive emotions, promotes resilience, and increases caring for others."[2]

One of the challenges is that we often equate care with immediate or specific intervention. "If you care, you'll do something and not only something, you'll do this…right now!" So when God doesn't act according to the way we think He should or within our timeframe, the foundation of a caring God can begin to crack and be replaced with a God who has failed and forgotten us in our time of need. In Psalm 13:1-2, out of desperation and grief, David doesn't beat around the bush. His words are about as straightforward as you could get and, in all honesty, borderline offensive.

> How long, O Lord? Will you forget me forever?
>   How long will you hide your face from me?
> How long must I take counsel in my soul
>   and have sorrow in my heart all the day?

It's one thing to believe God cares about us when life is great—the family is healthy, relationships are flourishing, career is moving along—and it's another thing to believe God cares about us when the lights go out, the rain starts to pour, and all we can see is a sky overtaken by what looks like a never-ending stream of gray clouds. So what's the answer? Has God forgotten you? Does God care or could He not care less? Maybe He cares, just not about this part of your life? These are questions often born from a hurting, maybe even confused, tired heart that wants a real answer, not a bandage imprinted with the words "it's always darkest before the dawn." No, sometimes it's dark and it stays that way for quite a while. Sometimes life is cruel and not at all what we expected and so the question of God's care grows louder and louder. This isn't unreasonable, this makes sense. One of my favorite lines from Brennan Manning probably isn't a favorite line for most. It comes toward the end of the first chapter in what I believe is one of the most significant books on grace in modern times, *The Ragamuffin Gospel*. In being brutally honest about the Christian life through the lens of the real world in which we live, he says, "For some, life is a long January."[3] I appreciate what Brennan says, not because it's encouraging by any stretch of the imagination but because it's true. It doesn't mean we're void of hope; it doesn't mean joy isn't within our grasp; it simply means life can be very challenging even for God's kids. In fact, He promised us it would be this way.

So does God care or has He in fact fallen asleep at the wheel of your life? Before we can answer this question appropriately, we need to take a minor detour because we have to reorient our way of thinking. I'll give fair warning, this might seem initially harsh or bitter because it pushes against our desire for quick resolution and challenges us to evaluate the strength and placement of our desires altogether, but, my friend, this is a good thing.

DESIRES AND DEMANDS

Good desires are just that, until they become demands. If God's care is predicated on Him meeting our demands, we will find ourselves time and time again on shaky ground. As Larry Crabb shares in his book *Shattered Dreams* (which I highly recommend),

> It's hard to hear, but it is important to know that God is not committed…to protecting us from agonizing problems that generate in our souls an experience that feels like death. We cannot count on God to arrange what happens in our lives in ways that will make us feel good.[4]

This doesn't mean that God doesn't care about our happiness or our circumstances, He absolutely does. The problem comes when we fall into the trap of pitting these two things, desire and circumstance, against each other. Let's stop and look at this very practically for a minute.

I desire…

- to have a spouse
- to have children and grow our family
- to be healed physically
- to be healed mentally
- to have stability
- to have my child healed physically/mentally
- To have resolution and healing from what happened in the past

If I were to ask you what all of these desires have in common, we would all agree: they're inherently good! None of these are evil. These are all good desires that we would expect God to be in agreement with. So what's the problem? On the surface there's absolutely no problem in praying and pleading with God to meet these good desires, to bring hopes and dreams to fruition. Only when our heartfelt pleading turns into unyielding demands do we find the path obstructed. As my friend Shelbi (who you'll hear about later) says, it's when we start treating God less like the cosmic creator and more like a cosmic vending machine we find ourselves in trouble. Once this shift in our heart takes place, we fall into the danger of handing over control to another ruler.

In the words of author Robert D. Jones, "Left unchecked, any desire has the potential to climb the stairs in an effort to overthrow and remove Jesus."[5] What does this have to do with God's care for us? Everything. When a good desire becomes a demand and that demand isn't met or resolved, the challenge of illusory truth steps in. Let me give you an example of what this looks like and how it plays out. I tell you at the early stages of your grief, "You know God cares." You agree. But the longer your desire goes unmet or the pain doesn't subside, this good desire can easily shift into a demand and you may start to ask, "Does God really care?" It may start as a question, but as more and more time goes by without any clear movement, it turns into an answer for the grief—"God doesn't care."

At a deeper level you may know full well this isn't true, but you may also function day-to-day as if it is. When the desire becomes the demand and the demand isn't met, questions and doubts make their way into the room and start to set up shop. All of a sudden our relationship with God moves from covenantal to contractual: "God, if you don't, then I won't." We start to hold back worship; we hold back adoration; we hold back prayers, we change the locks on our heart and refuse to answer His knock until we see the productivity we long for. We assume the role of general contractor, only willing to hand out proper payment once the job is complete.

If this were a sermon, this is the point where I would say to my church family, "don't miss this." There is nothing that can have a more detrimental and fracturing effect on our relationship with God than when the question of His care takes deep root and slowly becomes less of a question and more of a doubt. I'm not speaking hypothetically, I'm speaking from experience. I'm speaking as the thirty-three-year-old standing in the front row of the church, staring blankly at the beautiful stained glass window behind the baptismal on Green Lake Way, singing "Great is Thy Faithfulness" while simultaneously thinking "yeah, right… faithfulness." I've been there, many have been there and are there right now. The good news is that God, in His infinite kindness and grace, isn't surprised or shaken. He's not. Grieved on our behalf, yes. Shaken, no.

It's also not a coincidence that when our deepest desires go unmet, and God's care is in question, we can start to take detours. We start to take things into our own hands, we start to self-soothe, we start to look for care and resolution anywhere we can find it. When things are outside of our control we often reach for things that we believe we can control, no matter how unhealthy they might be. As our faith shakes, our heart begins an affair with whatever we believe might satisfy, even if only temporarily. And if that doesn't work, we simply retreat or go numb.

DEMANDS AND DETOURS

I don't think there's any better example of the progression from desire to demand to detour than in the story of Abraham and Sarah. Track with me. Here we find a couple with a great and good desire—to have a child. (God makes it abundantly clear that this is a good desire as He encourages people to "be fruitful and multiply" in Genesis 1:28.) The story of Abraham and Sarah picks up in Genesis 12 with them living peacefully in their homeland, when, out of the blue, God comes to them and says, "Pack up your things and leave everything you've ever known. I'm taking you somewhere completely new." And guess what? Abraham (then called Abram) believed God. He took Him at His word. That's significant. Sarah (then called Sarai), right by his side, shows the same radical faith and they embark on this mysterious journey.

So, they pack everything and set out. They find themselves in Harran, where Abram's father, Terah, passed away. It's a tough moment, no doubt. But Abram, Sarai, and their entourage, including their nephew Lot, keep moving, guided by God's promise. Picture their lives: no hotels, no GPS, just relying on God's guidance and living without the comforts we take for granted today.

Then a famine hits. They're forced to detour into Egypt to survive. Here, things get challenging. Abram, worried about Sarai's beauty—yes, beauty can be a blessing and a complication—asks her to say she's his sister. Technically true, but still quite deceptive. Pharaoh takes Sarai into his house, and Abram benefits materially—until God intervenes. Pharaoh catches on, realizing deception is afoot, and sends them packing, but not empty-handed. They head back, wealthier, but likely more reflective about such strategies.

Now, let's address the truly painful part: Sarai's barrenness. In their culture, this was distressing. It's not just personal but public—a source of shame. At this time Abraham and Sarah aren't just a little past childbearing age, Abraham is seventy-five. Their hopes and dreams have already been crushed. On paper and biologically, the family they hoped to have isn't happening. Yet God makes this audacious promise to Abram about his descendants being countless, as many as the stars lighting up the dark sky. "And he brought him outside and said, 'Look toward heaven, and number the stars, if you are able to number them.' Then he said to him, 'So shall your offspring be'" (Gen. 15:5). As Abraham and Sarah believe God, their good desire is brought back to life. Here's the problem: years pass and still no child. God, where are you? God, did you change your mind? God, have you gone silent? This doesn't seem like the actions, or inactions, of a good God. This doesn't seem to match up with the character of a God who cares for His kids. And, as so often happens, the good desire slips into a demand.

Sarah decides to take things into her own hands and proposes that Abraham conceive a child with her servant Hagar. Abraham agrees and a child is born. The problem is, while this was a cultural practice it definitely wasn't God's desire. Even during disobedience—and why I find this story so encouraging—God still isn't moved. He comes back to Abraham and reaffirms His promise: "And God said to Abraham, 'As for Sarai your wife, you shall not call her name Sarai, but Sarah shall be her name. I will bless her, and moreover, I will give you a son by her. I will bless her, and she shall become nations; kings of peoples shall come from her'" (Gen. 17:15-16). Abraham and Sarah laugh at the prospect of a ninety-year-old woman and a hundred-year-old man conceiving a child after decades of barrenness, and yet through the birth of Isaac God's promise is kept.

Look, I know that what you're walking with and through isn't easy to bear, far from it. I also know how confusing it can be when good desires go unmet. I know the pain and questioning of God's care that can come as you look around and see others having children, getting married, building community, moving forward, not struggling in the same way or with the same grief. I know that this is often accompanied by the feeling of being alone, one of the greatest fears for all of humanity. I know all too well the temptation to run from God to something that you believe will satisfy, to allow a new ruler to take hold of your heart. To search for care somewhere else, but always coming up empty and unfulfilled. Like a small child running away from home, only to get a few blocks down the street before turning and coming back to the people who love him.

What do we do when God doesn't care for us in the way we hope, think, or expect that He should? What do we do when His timeline and provision isn't our timeline and provision? With even the smallest thread of faith remaining, we tighten our grip on Jesus. I know, I know, this can seem overly simplistic but it's absolutely true. There is so much happening behind the scenes that we aren't privy to in God's care that we have to resort to faith and trust. I'm reminded of these words from John Piper, "In EVERY situation and EVERY circumstance of your life, God is always doing a thousand different things that you cannot see and you do not know."[6] One of my favorite lines in all of the Bible comes from one of Jesus' most intense and wayward disciples, Peter. In John 6, Jesus has just challenged His crowd of followers that in order to follow Him they'll have to fully embrace Him as the Bread of Life, or else turn and walk away. Imagine this scene: people in droves walking away from the actual Messiah, even after He fed them and a few thousand more with a couple of fish and some bread, healed people, and even walked on water for good measure. As the crowd leaves, Jesus, in a moment of tenderness, turns to His twelve misfit disciples and asks the same question He asks you and me as we sit with the most uninvited and often irreconcilable grief: "Do you want to go away as well?" Peter's answer on behalf of the other disciples is so beautifully honest and simple, "Lord, to whom shall we go? You have the words of eternal life" (vv. 67-68). Peter had no idea what was coming, he had no idea how hard things would get, but he clung on to faith and trust. For God to still be good in the midst of the pain means He is operating with great purpose and care. This truth rises above our feelings. We'll get to the purpose part in a few chapters. For now I want to encourage and challenge us that we have to be so careful not to tightly bind our desired movement from God to the determining factor of God's care for us. These two things can, and often do, look different in the muddiness of life.

RETHINKING CARE

When a parent doesn't show up on an important day, it's a big deal. I learned this in third grade. My friend Derick had a difficult relationship with his father. His parents were divorced and meaningful time with his dad was something Derick valued more than anything. Even as a third grader I knew this because of how much he talked about his dad and would share how amazing he was over peanut butter and jellies in the cafeteria. So when Parents' Day rolled around, Derick was bouncing off the walls because his dad promised he would be there. Unfortunately, that promise wasn't kept. I watched joy turn to sorrow and then to a complete emotional breakdown. Derick was inconsolable and his mom had to take him home early. As I think back on this now, some thirty years later, something very clear comes to the surface. My young friend didn't need his father to *do* anything for him, he just needed him to *be* present. More than anything, Derick just wanted his father to be there with him. This really is the heartbeat of genuine, authentic care. This is why we're seeing a movement in our current generation of fathers being more present with their children. According to a recent study, fathers are now spending three times more time with their children than their fathers before them.[7] This is a significant culture shift that reflects a gospel value.

Presence is primary when it comes to care. Not simply swooping in and out and solving problems, but ongoing presence born out of a deep-seated love for another. This doesn't mean movement isn't important, but it balances what can easily become out of balance, especially when movement isn't easily identifiable. This is why God's promise is not that life will be hard and He'll fix all of it this side of heaven. No, life will be hard and He'll be *with you* through all of it. Like a parent holding a child's hand through a dark forest, offering comfort and the ever-present reminder that they are not alone, God makes it clear and says to us, I will hold your hand through whatever life throws at you: "[I]will not leave you or forsake you" (Deut. 31:6, 8).

From the cool of the garden in Eden, through the deserts leading away from Egypt, to the streets filled with people searching for hope, God has walked with us. In the greatest show of care, He has even come to live among us as Emmanuel "God with us," and walked *for* us where we dared not go.

A NEEDED ASSURANCE

With that, my friend, allow this truth to break through the lie: God hasn't stopped caring for one second. You've never not been on His mind. In fact, He knows every single tear you've cried over this crushed hope, dream, or desire. Hear these words from Psalm 56:8 as gentle assurance. "You keep track of all my sorrows. You have collected all my tears in your bottle. You have recorded each one in your book." (NLT). God hasn't turned a blind eye to your pain. He hasn't walked out on you when you need Him most. It's the exact opposite. He knows every sadness you've felt, every tear you've cried. He's been there in the room with you when it felt overwhelming, in the car when you had to pull over to soak the steering wheel in tears. He has seen it all and kept it close, and He's keeping track of it. He not only cares, He grieves with you, He hasn't left you, and He will have the final word of vindication over your pain and loss. When it's hard to believe (and believe me, I know how hard it can be) and His care is in question, go to the cross again and again and be reminded. What may feel like a lack of intervention is not a sign of His lack of affection. Be reminded that the one who was crushed *for* you without a doubt cares about what feels crushing *to* you. As we see in Isaiah 41:13, God not only cares, but He is also holding our hand through it all. "For I, the LORD your God, hold your right hand; it is I who say to you, 'Fear not, I am the one who helps you.'"

Any time we question God's care, this can be accompanied with fear. What if this is a sign that I don't have the kind of relationship with God I thought I had? While this question makes sense and may scream loudly in our head and heart, allow God's grace and sovereignty to be even louder. Earlier we referenced Jesus, the crowd, and Peter. What we didn't touch on is something Jesus says that is meant to offer assurance to our unsettled and grieving hearts. "No one can come to me unless the Father who sent me draws him" (John 6:44). In essence, it's God who has drawn you to faith in Christ, and therefore it's God (not you) that keeps you secure in Christ. You can doubt, you can question, and yet you remain completely secure. You are no less secure on your greatest day of doubt than you are on your strongest day of faith. I love these words of the late Tim Keller: "It is not the strength of your faith but the object of your faith that saves you."[8] I would go so far as to add "and sustains you." Every tear; every moment of sadness; every sorrow. He cares. Your pain is not lost on Him, as we'll look at in the next chapter. Nothing you can share with Him, no amount of emotion, nothing is too much for Him to handle.

Let's wrap up this section with this encouragement from Pete Greig from his book *God on Mute* as it is a great summation of this part of our conversation.

> When we are scared and hurting, when life feels chaotic and out of control, it is more important than ever to anchor ourselves in the absolute and eternal truth that we are dearly loved and deeply held by the most powerful being in the universe. Let this be the great non-negotiable in our lives, the platform for all our other thoughts, and the plumbline for our prayers.[9]

REFLECTIONS

1. Why do feelings play such a large part when it comes to believing we are being cared for? How can this become unhealthy?

2. Has your good desire become a demand? If so, what would it look like to put the desire in its proper place?

3. Look back at Psalm 56:8 and Isaiah 41:13. How do these assurances encourage you, and where is there still tension?

PART 2

WHAT WE PICK UP

4

IT'S OKAY TO NOT BE OKAY

In the first chapter of this book I opened up about the struggle of infertility Laura and I faced. This was the invisible grief that was dropped into our lives. I also shared that it took me three years to actually sit with the pain and loss in an honest way, without running (either to quick solutions or alcohol) or laughing it off to avoid actually feeling much at all. So what happened three years later? A friend asked if I would drive him to the airport. I readily agreed, even though I remember it had been a really, really hard day. I had gone for a run earlier around Green Lake Park near our home. It was July, which meant it was absolutely beautiful weather in Seattle, not a cloud in sight. I had made it a point to avoid running by the playground and seeing all of the parents with little ones laughing and playing. I must have lost track of where I was in the park (I am, and will forever be, directionally challenged) and pretty soon I found myself at the playground. Don't get me wrong, I am 100 per cent pro-family, but it had become increasingly painful to observe the joy others were experiencing when we wanted so desperately to experience it ourselves. So yeah, a tough day.

I picked up my friend and we started toward the airport, casually talking about soccer and how crowded the city became during this time of year. As I pulled off the highway he said, "I have some news to share." I didn't need to hear anything else; I knew exactly what he was going to share. He and his wife, who were at least five years younger than Laura and myself, had decided to start trying for a child literally two months before. "We're pregnant!" This was great, it really was. New life is amazing and wonderful. I was so happy for them and at the same time felt so crushed inside.

I pulled up to the curb, gave him a hug, and drove off. I should have gone straight home but I didn't. Instead I pulled into a gas station, went in, and bought a six-pack. I didn't want to feel this, I just wanted to be numb. I drank the first beer, popped open the second and finished that one off in a matter of minutes. It didn't help. Why wasn't this helping? In fact, I remember quite vividly that the opposite started to happen. I started to feel so incredibly sad and angry and then shameful. Not shame for drinking in the parking lot of a gas station, shame because I couldn't give Laura the family we wanted. I started to visualize children that would never exist and it was all too much. It felt like my heart was being hit with a burst of water from a fire hose. I turned the ignition, got back on the highway and as I started to cross the bridge back into north Seattle on I-5, a thought came into my mind. It wasn't just a thought, it was an actual consideration. As I drove among the cars and trucks, flooded with manic emotions and tears streaming down my face, I thought, "Maybe I should drive straight into the median and give Laura a shot at a family with someone else." I had never had a thought like this but it was as real and visceral as they come. In that moment the pain became so intense that escape put on a false mask of freedom. As real as this thought was and as much as I seriously considered it, I soon found myself back in my driveway. Before going inside I sat there for a moment, gripping the wheel in a cold sweat.

The house was empty and I went straight up to our second floor, closed the door to the dark guest room, lay face down on the carpet, and cried. This was my dark night of the soul. I could either continue in this slow-motion suicide of drinking away my feelings and refusing to face what was happening, or I could give in. Not give in to myself, but give in to the one who had been calling me back home. I was a broken prodigal who made the liquor cabinet my church and worshiped there almost every night. My anti-spiritual gift was laughing the pain away and the profound ability to wear masks of strength and resilience. But through it all, the Father never wavered from standing at the door and keeping lookout for His son. I was finally broken but, for the first time in a long time, I was broken in the right way. I couldn't keep running, I didn't have the strength. Something had to change. In what felt like the darkest moment of my existence, I also felt the most calming presence reassuring me of one thing: "you're not alone, I'm here." No, I've never heard the audible voice of God, but I knew with certainty, for the first time in a long time, that although I had been running, He was right there.

Over the next few days I reached out to two people: a therapist, and a retired Anglican priest who counseled pastors. I've wrestled with anxiety since high school and have had occasional panic attacks (still do), but I had never been to a counselor or a therapist and I had mixed feelings about going. But I knew I needed help and I knew I needed to talk to someone with outside perspective. Some people will tell you that if you just trust God, have more faith and rely on the Holy Spirit's power within you, you don't need to medicate and you don't need therapy. Chances are that, although these individuals may be speaking from conviction, they are also speaking more from a place of conception, not a place of lived experience. I find this way of thinking is not only unhelpful and untrue, but salt in the wound of those who are hurting, struggling, and in need of help. Mental illness is real, anxiety is real, depression is real, suicidal ideations are real. For two immensely relatable biblical characters, David and Paul, anxiety and depression are common themes in their lives. Look at David's words in Psalm 31,

> Be merciful to me, LORD, for I am in distress;
>   my eyes grow weak with sorrow,
>   my soul and body with grief.
> My life is consumed by anguish
>   and my years by groaning;
> my strength fails because of my affliction,
>   and my bones grow weak (vv. 9-10, NIV)

Yes, David is clearly depressed. As he says, the weight of his grief has essentially consumed him. This is a man after God's own heart; this is a man who had incredible faith. But he was also just a man. I want to encourage you as a pastor and as someone who knows what it is to be anxious and at times depressed: don't keep this to yourself. If you feel like the pain and loss is too much and you aren't sure you can keep going, don't allow shame to write the next pages of your life. You have people who love you, and a God who loves you. It's okay to not be okay, but it's not okay to keep it to yourself. If you broke your arm I would assume you would go to the doctor to get it reset, so why would we not ask for the gift of help when something breaks within?

Over the next several months I would meet once a week with the therapist and once a week with the retired priest. Both were incredibly helpful in their own unique ways. I did not want to take this path. There were days I wanted to cancel the appointment and go back to the old way of doing things. But for the first time in three years I was willing to stop running and bend my knee to the God who sat with me in the dark and reminded me I wasn't alone. Although it took me a while to warm up, I started to really enjoy my conversations with Dr. Dover, a seventy-eight-year-old retired priest who had dedicated his life to helping others. After the passing of his wife Susan, he decided to join a counseling hub out of Kent, Washington and walk with other pastors in their journey.

He shared something with me during our second session that has always stuck with me and I often find myself sharing it with others. He shared this during the second session because the first was essentially me rambling through partially-pieced-together thoughts that I wasn't sure made any sense, while at the same time attempting to present myself as someone I wasn't—emotionally in-tune and overwhelmingly stable. I was none of these things; I was a mess and he saw right through me. Luckily he was well-versed in pastors trying to outwardly present a concrete foundation while on the inside feeling like the most fragile piece of glass, ready to shatter at the slightest jolt. He reminded me that this was going to be a process, one we would take together a step at a time as long as one rule was followed, that rule being honesty. Unfiltered, unpolished, honesty. With that, we made it to our second session.

I arrived at the counseling center, sat in the small but cozy waiting area and was soon greeted by Dr. Dover. We sat down in his office. He pulled out a piece of paper, not to write on but to use as an illustration. "Drew, think of this piece of paper as your faith before infertility." He then tore part of the paper. "When something unusually painful and unexpected drops into our life, something that isn't easily resolved, it's easy for that paper faith to tear. It doesn't mean it's completely torn apart but it is torn. Maybe for the first time in your life it puts what you have claimed to believe about God, His character, and His plans to the test." I knew exactly what he meant.This was one of the new realities I felt but was too stubborn, or maybe too scared, to face. "You can either see this as a bad thing or see it as an opportunity to face the questions, face the doubts, face the emotions, and develop a stronger, more concrete faith that isn't easily shaken." This all sounded great, but it also sounded uncomfortable—not the quick fix I was hoping for. In his second work on the topic, *A Grief Observed,* C.S. Lewis shares, "You never know how much you really believe anything until its truth or falsehood becomes a matter of life and death to you."[1] I just wanted to move on. I wanted to "get better," but it was becoming clear that God wanted to move something in me.

Up until this point, the idea of bringing to God the emotions I had been burying, doubts I had been suppressing, and questions I had been avoiding, was unthinkable. Although I knew God to be relational, I struggled to see that relationship as truly familial and open to challenging dialogue. In a men's study last year one of the participants asked about the balance between viewing God as "my homeboy" and, on the other end of the spectrum, as an unapproachable king. One lacked reverence and awe, and the other lacked accessibility and heartfelt connection. I knew I was much too formal in my approach. I would soon realize this was completely fear-based. I was afraid that being truly honest with God—for better, worse, and everything in between—would be disrespectful and a sign of dishonoring doubt. I was operating as if God was a furrowed-browed boss who only cared about the end result, not as a loving Father who grieved with His hurting children.

"Drew, it's okay to not be okay and it's okay to share that with God, because I know and you know, He is too kind to leave you there." With these words from this kind man, emotions came flooding out. Tears that had been stored up for who knows how long flowed like a river of freedom from my tired and knotted heart. Over the following weeks and months, and even to this day, brutally honest conversations with God would take place. Once I fully embraced that God is not in the business of hiring workers, but of adopting sons and daughters, I felt the security and invitation to be completely open. If I knew that I was secure in my relationship with Christ, that it was unchanging no matter what, then why not walk through the doors of honesty and vulnerability that afforded? Not only can God handle it, like a good Father He welcomes it. I began to press in to the idea that God's ears are always open, even when our hearts are unfiltered.

I mentioned above that C.S. Lewis has written two books on the topic of grief (both highly recommended). The first, *The Problem of Pain,* written twenty-one years before Lewis experienced the profound personal loss of his wife, is a more academic and philosophical examination of the problem of suffering and pain from a Christian perspective. Lewis aimed to reconcile the existence of suffering with the idea of a benevolent God. The second, *A Grief Observed,* is much more raw and emotive in its discussion on the loss of his wife. One philosophical, the other personal. One objective, the other subjective. One looking at grief as a concept, the other based on lived experience. In the very first line of

A Grief Observed, he says something that taps into the very heart of those walking through grief. "No one ever told me that grief felt so like fear."[2] It was this fear that controlled me for years. It was fear that made deep roots and ran in ten different directions. I had been so scared by the grief and then scared about what would happen if I faced the grief. But here's what I experienced: honesty with God and myself didn't push God away—it drew me closer. The more I opened up, the more I realized my desperate need for God. I couldn't survive the valley of the shadow of death on my own strength. If healing was in the future, no matter what the future looked like I knew fear couldn't call the shots. Instead, it had to be about stepping into that honest, raw relationship with the God I believe cares and listens. This had to win the day.

Over the years, these soul conversations have unfolded wherever the journey has taken me. I have prayed prayers of desperation and supplication. Picture this: sitting in the car, voice raised in raw anger, crying out to the heavens, "How is this good? Why won't you mend this broken body of mine?" Then there are those nights, when the world is wrapped in silence and the heart chokes on sadness and numbness: "I hate these feelings. The weight is too much! Where are you?" On sidewalks and dirt paths, I've poured out my heart, wrestling with the tough questions, daring to expose my doubts: "You've called this desire good, so why do you hold back from fulfilling it?" Real relationships are messy but they're also honest. Through all of it, the most helpful truth that will bring us to, and keep us in, a place of honest connectedness is knowing that we have a savior and friend who can relate.

JESUS CAN RELATE

> For we do not have a high priest who is unable to sympathize with our weaknesses (Heb. 4:15a).

In Jesus we not only have God taking on flesh, but we also have God living in the muck and mire of the human experience. Through the life of Jesus, God presents us with yet another gift of grace, this time in the form of relatability. For us to be relentlessly vulnerable with God, our hearts hunger for a relatable friend. The author of Hebrews makes it clear when he uses the word "sympathize." There is only one way to learn sympathy, as shown in the Greek root of the word, *pathos*, and that's "to feel or suffer with."[3] What a great reminder that not only can God handle all of my messy and sometimes disjointed emotions, He also fully understands them. He is not detached and distant. For those of us who sometimes struggle with falling back into the notion of God as cosmically distant, this helps keep that in check. Practically speaking, any time you feel this temptation slipping in, I would strongly suggest flipping to the Gospel of John and soaking up the life of Jesus in a very day-to-day sense. We need the reminder that He walked like we walk; He got tired like we get tired; His feet hurt like our feet hurt; He tasted salt and had a thirst for water like we do; He had personal relationships with all of their complications like we have; and, yes, He faced pain and loss like we face pain and loss, but even more so.

- Jesus experienced joy (John 15:10-11).
- Jesus experienced physical and emotional exhaustion (Matt. 14:13; Mark 6:31; Luke 5:16; John 6:15).
- Jesus experienced righteous anger (Matt. 23:33).

- Jesus experienced sadness and sorrow (John 11:33-35).
- Jesus experienced compassion (Matt. 9:20-22, John 8:1-11).
- Jesus experienced frustration (Matt. 17:14-20; Mark 4:35-41).
- Jesus experienced agony (Luke 22:42).

Jesus didn't live a life devoid of honest emotions or protected from uncomfortable feelings. And when it comes to being able to relate to us in our grief, we are in good company. "He was despised and rejected—a man of sorrows, acquainted with deepest grief" (Isa. 53:3, NLT).

We can buy into the false idea that Jesus, as 100 per cent human and 100 per cent God, would flip on some sort of God-switch in order to rise above human limitations, to perform miracles, or avoid pain, but this simply isn't the case. Philippians 2:6 confirms this, saying that Christ Jesus "though he was in the form of God, did not count equality with God a thing to be grasped." Every miracle performed, every temptation resisted, every sorrow felt, every agony endured, all was from a place of complete reliance on the Holy Spirit. Not some Christological magic trick, not a phone-a-friend to His Father.

THE WAY OF DAVID

I love a good movie, I have for as long as I can remember. I'm not at the level of my brother Joel or cousin Matt who are cinema aficionados, but I appreciate great writing and directing nonetheless. It was actually my oldest brother Troy who introduced me to one of my top ten films, *The Apostle*, starring and directed by Robert Duvall. In this 1997 classic, Sonny (played by Duvall) is a Pentecostal preacher in Texas who has built his life and reputation around his charismatic preaching. However, his life takes a turn when he discovers that his wife, Jessie (played by Farrah Fawcett), is having an affair with a young minister at their church. In a fit of rage, Sonny confronts his wife's lover during a baseball game, and in the heat of the moment, he ends up seriously injuring him with a baseball bat, which leads to the man being put into a coma. Faced with the potential of being caught by the authorities, Sonny flees and goes to live with his mother. He abandons his previous identity and chooses to start anew, introducing himself as "The Apostle E.F." to symbolize his commitment to seeking a fresh start.

There's a memorable scene in the movie filled with power and intensity as Sonny yells at God over the path his life has taken. Overwhelmed with anger, frustration, and desperation, Sonny vents his emotions with raw honesty as he wrestles with his faith and circumstances. A concerned neighbor hears all of the commotion and makes their way to the house where Sonny's mother offers up this explanation. "That's my son, that is. I'll tell ya: ever since he was an itty bitty boy, sometimes he talks to the Lord and sometimes he yells at the Lord. Tonight, he just happens to be yellin' at Him."[4]

This scene immediately transports me to some of David's most intense conversations with the God he loved. This is the approach I would encourage us to take as we have ongoing conversations like this along our journey of grief. The man after God's own heart didn't waver when it came to sharing honest emotion and asking raw, heartfelt questions. Here are a few examples:

> How long, O LORD? Will you forget me forever? How long will you hide your face from me? (Ps. 13:1)
>
> My God, my God, why have you forsaken me? (Ps. 22:1)

Why, O Lord, do you stand far away? Why do you hide yourself in times of trouble? (Ps. 10:1)

Here's what I want us to notice about David's conversations with God: He starts with honesty. He shares what he's feeling, what he's thinking, his questions, and even his doubts. He knows his relationship with God is secure and he knows God welcomes his cries. Like any good father, God doesn't want His children to pretend to be okay when their heart aches. He doesn't want us to go inward to self-pity or self-denial; He wants us to outwardly express to Him where we are and how we are. This doesn't mean we don't have reverence toward God. What this means is that we are diving deeply into the profound intimacy of a genuine, palpable relationship with the creator of all that is, fully known and no longer hidden from Him.

While David often begins these conversations with brutal honesty, I want us to also see that this is never a one-sided conversation. In fact, God is the one who has the first voice. Whenever we commune with God, whenever we pray, we are always the second voice. In His boundless wisdom and tender kindness, God has already spoken through His Word. Overflowing with grace and truth, the Bible is an intimate revelation of His heart. We then have the opportunity to respond to Him as life takes shape. This is what we see with David and this is what God invites us into.

What I appreciate about David's approach is that even in his pain he always allows God to be the final voice. This doesn't change his circumstance and it doesn't change his plea, but it does serve as a constant reminder and assurance. By bringing God back into the conversation, what David is doing is expressing faith and trust amidst all of the mess. He's assuming that God is still good and knows what He's doing. Look at how David ends all of the same chapters we used as examples:

But I have trusted in your steadfast love; my heart shall rejoice in your salvation. I will sing to the LORD, because he has dealt bountifully with me. (Ps. 13:5-6)

From you comes my praise in the great congregation; my vows I will perform before those who fear him. The afflicted shall eat and be satisfied; those who seek him shall praise the LORD! (Ps. 22:25-26)

O LORD, you hear the desire of the afflicted; you will strengthen their heart; you will incline your ear. (Ps. 10:17)

I love this. It's so good. God, this is what I feel, but I know who you are. God, this is what I think, but I believe you're still good. God, I don't know where you are or what you're doing but I believe you hear my cry. I believe this is a godly approach that provides healthy guardrails. If, on reflection, you believe some of these conversations crossed a line, confess, repent, and walk in grace.

Friend, God is inviting us to lay bare our pain and loss. In this sacred vulnerability, we find that His acceptance eclipses our fear and His grace covers all.

REFLECTIONS

1. Are there any unhealthy coping mechanisms or trauma behaviors you've been pressing in to? What do you believe is at the core of this?

2. Why are we tempted to believe it's not okay to not be okay?

3. How does it help to know that Jesus can relate? How should this open the door to being raw, open, and honest with God about what we're feeling and experiencing?

5

THE GIFT OF GRIEF

MEET SARAH

How can something so painful produce anything good? This is a legitimate question and one that Sarah alluded to on a gray Tuesday morning at a local coffee shop. "Seriously, Drew, I feel like everyone else I know is moving forward in life and I'm just watching the years go by...wasted." Sarah had just turned thirty-two and with this birthday came another hard break-up. They were starting to pile up. As we sat there sipping our coffee, Sarah recounted a story that we had talked through on several occasions. The past ten years of her life since graduating college read like a laundry list of failed relationships. "All I want is to find a nice guy that I can start a family with, is that really too much to ask?" I could feel myself start to plead with God on her behalf: "Her desire isn't selfish or off-base, it's actually something *you* said is a good thing!"

If we zoomed out a bit, from the outside looking in Sarah's life seemed very attractive. She graduated top of her class from the University of Washington (go Huskies!), had a great job in the career of her choice, and had a solid group of friends and tight-knit gospel community. And yet, this one good desire continued to go unmet. A desire that not only consumed her thoughts and pulled at her heart but also pulled her back to the dark corridor of an abusive childhood. When Sarah was in middle school she was sexually abused by a family member and, instead of ensuring she received the support she needed, her parents chose to bury the incident and downplay its trauma, an unfortunate yet fairly typical response to familial abuse. This obviously had intense and long-reaching effects on Sarah, both physiologically and emotionally. Thank God, as an adult Sarah was able to recognize the gaping, open wound that was causing her to walk with a pretty significant relational limp. She started to see a therapist and over the following two years began to heal in seismic and transformative ways—and then she met a great guy and lived happily ever after, right? Wrong. Because real life for 99.9 per cent of us isn't an old-school Disney movie; things often aren't that simple. In fact, it's usually outright messy and exacerbated in cases of trauma and pain.

Although Sarah had worked through her past and had even come to the place of forgiving her abuser and parents, (talk about grace) there still seemed to be these lingering questions in the back of her mind. "Is there something wrong with me? Am I too damaged for someone to want to be with me? Is it my fault I'm not married yet?" With every dating relationship that would come and go, these questions grew louder and louder, and with them the lie that all of these years had been a waste. We'll get to this more in a minute but I want you to highlight those two words, "a waste." Seriously, draw a line, pull out a highlighter, whatever you need to do. This is a fundamental deception and one we need to unpack and take a flamethrower to—but more on that in a minute.

As we sat and talked for the next hour about what went sideways in this latest dating disaster, Sarah's eyes welled up with tears as she shared how in the beginning things looked so great, so promising. It had been like being wrapped in a warm blanket after coming in from the cold, but things took a turn a few months later and, like so many relationships before, he became distant and disinterested, only further perpetuating and fueling the question "is there something wrong with me?" Not only did each failed relationship re-open the door for this looming question, but they also whispered, "what a waste." As her pastor and as a friend I listened carefully and intently and started to discern what I was hearing at the heart of her words. Once Sarah finished sharing, I remember looking at her and saying, "I want you to know something. Something I'll keep telling you as long as you need to hear it. It's not your fault, and you're not damaged goods. God loves you, and *none* of these years have been wasted. I know it's been a long, painful road, and I affirm that your desire is a good one. I know you didn't ask for it, but there's a gift in this grief." Sarah's eyes met mine with a half smirking look of disgust, and then she said, "A gift? If this is a gift, can I return it?"

Grief as a gift is a hard pill to swallow, especially when you're fully immersed in it. It doesn't square well with the fragility of our hearts or make any sense on paper. The idea that what may very well be the most painful reality or season in our lives is a gift from our heavenly Father can seem very foreign and, honestly, pretty offensive. This is probably the hardest chapter in this entire book to put down on paper because even as I'm writing it I feel the pushback in my own heart. So, before you get too offended and log on to Amazon to give this a one-star review, let me explain.

NEW EYES

It was probably a year ago that I found myself watching YouTube video after YouTube video, not of cats playing pianos or dogs speaking (I knew that's what you were thinking, and yes I have gone down that rabbit trail on occasion) but of blind people receiving eye transplants and experiencing vision for the first time. It was amazing to witness the raw emotion and overwhelming, speechless joy of these individuals. As tears streamed down their faces it didn't take a rocket scientist to understand that their lives were forever changed. I even found myself getting outwardly emotional for these people I'd never met because their joy was so pure and unscripted. They literally had a new insight that they had never had before. Certain experiences were once out of their grasp; now, for the first time, they experienced a new, awe-inspiring reality.

As we journey through grief, whatever the circumstance may be, our vision is forever altered. There are things you are now able to see and process that you were never able to do before. As Mary Francis O'Connor, leading psychologist in the study of grief and the brain, states, "grieving is a form of learning."[1] God, in His intricate wiring of our very beings, not only allows us to learn how to co-mingle with our grief to the point that it's not completely debilitating, but He also enables us to learn or re-learn how to steward what matters most and what matters less in unique and profound ways. Because of your experience of invisible grief, you will be able to interact with and care for others experiencing suffering, and do so in ways that are uniquely insightful, helpful, and healing and with an empathy that most who have not walked this road cannot.

NEW APPRECIATION

Believe it or not, this unique gift of grief is born out of appreciation. No, not an appreciation for the pain. Remember, 1 Thessalonians 5:18 says "give thanks *in* all circumstances" not *for* all circumstances (emphasis added). No, this is a different kind of appreciation, similar to how certain animals with poor eyesight have a heightened sense of smell. When we experience seasons or circumstances of grief, we have a heightened sense of God-given appreciation born out of the painful circumstance or unmet desire in our lives. Where we may see others take certain relationships, realities, health, etc. for granted, we resolve never to take these things for granted; they're far too valuable to us because, in the waiting and wandering through the desert of grief, a unique appreciation has been building and maturing, regardless of whether we see these desires come to fruition or not. Let me use an example.

In the vast majority of the western world clean drinking water isn't something we are concerned about, and lacking water isn't even a blip on our mental map. In all the years of stumbling into the kitchen half asleep at midnight and turning on the faucet, I've never once thought, "What if there's no water?" I have never had an emotional reaction at the sight of water, and I've never offered up prayers thanking God for water (although that's not a bad idea). But imagine you were dropped in the Sahara Desert for a week without any water in sight and no timetable for availability or rescue. Suddenly, everything changes. Imagine journeying over hill after hill of sandy landscape as the dry desert wind paints the side of your face, your mouth dry and lips chapped as your eyes, red from the sand and wind, struggle to stay open. You're not sure how much longer you can keep going but with your eyes barely able to make out the path ahead you see something. There in the distance—it's a town! You see people, which means they must have water! You muster one last physical push and run toward the people, and there you're greeted with a cool cup of water fresh from a well. As the water hits your lips you fall to your wind-worn knees, tears streaming as you thank God for this one life-altering, life-giving drink. You are completely overjoyed and completely overwhelmed. You realize at that moment that you will never look at a glass of water the same again. For every day after this, there will be a newfound appreciation for what you once took for granted.

NEW ABILITIES

No matter where you are in the journey of invisible grief, this "learning" that Mary Francis O'Connor referenced is taking place. You are receiving, or have received, new eyes. You can relate in new ways, discern in new ways, listen in new ways, understand in new ways, offer encouragement in new ways, and speak non-platitude-ridden truth in new ways. Your grief is a gift, both inwardly and outwardly. It's a gift for you and a gift for others. It's a gift that slams the door in the face of "what a waste." No, it's not a gift you asked for, but it's a gift that carries incredible power, and it should be held and treated with great care. It's a gift that desperately needs to be shared with other tired, confused, searching souls. It's a gift that should be opened and used now, not put on the shelf to gather dust for the future when things are better, different, or fully processed. This is what the Apostle Paul embodied and lived out when it came to his own pain and suffering. It's also why so many of us resonate with his life and his teaching. He was flawed, had a past that he grieved, faced real pain and loss, but Paul was brutally honest about it, and he not only had hope, but was also able to share that hope with others. He accepted the uninvited gift of hardship, pain, and, at times, sorrow and longing, and he didn't waste it. Look at 2 Corinthians 12 with me for a moment.

> A thorn was given me in the flesh, a messenger of Satan to harass me, to keep me from becoming conceited. Three times I pleaded with the Lord about this, that it should leave me. But he said to me, "My grace is sufficient for you, for my power is made perfect in weakness." Therefore I will boast all the more gladly of my weaknesses, so that the power of Christ may rest upon me (2 Cor. 12:7b-9).

Paul didn't know why God gave him this "thorn"; he didn't ask for it. In fact, he asked that it would be taken away three times, but to no avail. How many times have we laid awake at night, hearts filled with sorrow, staring at the ceiling and asking God to change the circumstance: to bring the spouse, bring the baby, heal the depression and anxiety, heal the phobia, take away the loneliness? To take it a step further, whatever this "thorn" was—physical, spiritual, or mental it wasn't the only thing Paul had to endure. Just a chapter earlier he opens up about the pain he's had to face since becoming a follower of Jesus.

Paul was whipped, beaten, stoned, and shipwrecked; danger was all around him; he experienced exhausting labor and hardship; he was sleepless, hungry, thirsty, without food, exposed to the elements; he faced daily pressure and anxiety for his churches (2 Cor. 11:24-28).

Among all of these circumstances and seasons, what was ahead for Paul is even worse. (I know, right!) He would spend years in cold, dark prisons, completely isolated from the outside world. It would have been understandable, if not expected, for Paul's situational pain to boil over into anger, doubt, and depression and for Paul to become numb and distant from that time forward. It would have been easy for Paul to say "what a waste." Yet, what we see is the complete opposite; what we see is resolve born out of grace. It was this grace *in* the pain that allowed Paul to pen some of the most hopeful, God-inspired letters that would reach far beyond the churches of that time to you and me today. There is no doubt that through the incredible pain and struggle, Paul received new perspective and abilities to minister to other malnourished hope-seekers like you and me. When so much was stripped away, a newfound clarity and appreciation for the importance of grace, forgiveness, and endurance emerged, all wrapped in a unique love for the church and palatable relatability mirroring Jesus Himself, "a man of sorrows, and acquainted with grief" (Isa. 53:3).

We don't just see this with Paul; we see this throughout the tapestry of the biblical narrative. We see this in the story of Joseph, who is sold into slavery by his brothers and experiences intense suffering and loss. Through his grief, his character is honed. Stripped of everything familiar, he learns resilience and integrity, and he learns to completely rely on God. Joseph's grief becomes his unique strength. When called upon by the king, the very suffering he endured is what enabled him to respond with empathy and insight during Egypt's crisis. His new ability to navigate complexity informed his approach to store grain during years of abundance, a direct result of his seasoned, tested character born out of his personal pain. In Ruth we witness a woman in a foreign land who loses everything as her husband, his brother, and her father-in-law pass away. Yet it's through her grief that she is able to care for her mother-in-law in a profound and meaningful way.

Still not sure whether this gift is a good thing? I understand, so let's take it straight to the source. I want you to take a few moments to think about this reality. Without grief there is no gospel, there is no good news, there is no lasting hope for you and me. Without Jesus enduring pain and sorrow, rejection from a people He came to save, blood-soaked tears in the garden, denial from friends, separation from the Father, and the cruelty of the cross, we would be utterly hopeless and alone. The greatest grief that's ever been borne results in the greatest gift to you and to me, the gift of new and eternal life.

NOTHING IS WASTED

Although Laura and I have wrestled with many doubts over the years, especially related to the grief of our infertility, one of the things we believe at a visceral level is that God is at work in the life of His kids, even in the dark. Throughout the pain and loss, He's working to give you new insight, a new appreciation, and new abilities. This is at least part of the purpose in the pain. We'll take a deep dive into this in a few chapters.

As God works in you, He wants to work through you. "Blessed be the God and Father of our Lord Jesus Christ, the Father of mercies and God of all comfort, who comforts us in all our affliction, so that we may be able to comfort those who are in any affliction, with the comfort with which we ourselves are comforted by God" (2 Cor. 1:3-4). Through this circumstance or season, He's gifting you with the ability to connect with care for, and relate to other wounded sheep at the right time, in the right place, and in ways that many others can't. Through any and all discouragement, be encouraged in this: I can assure you this isn't a wasted season in your life. In God's economy, nothing is wasted.

It's been ten years since Sarah and I had that conversation at that small coffee shop, but it still sticks with me.

I remember about a year later connecting with Sarah in the church hallway. As we were talking she said, "I get the gift." It didn't resonate with me at first. Sarah smiled. "You know, the gift I couldn't return." Over the years Sarah has walked with countless young women through their own invisible grief, passing on the gift that, although she didn't ask for it, has been used in a truly beautiful and redemptive way, with not a single teardrop wasted.

REFLECTIONS

1. How has your grief been a gift to others? How could it be?

2. How has God given you new eyes, new appreciation, and new abilities through your grief?

3. How does the idea that nothing is wasted help to re-frame your perspective on the grief you're walking with?

6

A BETTER IDENTITY

I faced my first identity crisis in the third grade while attending Blue Ridge Elementary. Back in the nineties kids were ruthless about wearing the right brands, especially when it came to shoes. I knew this coming out of the summer of 1992 and was determined to do anything in my power to make sure I started school wearing one of the big three brands on my feet. I didn't care if it was Nike, Reebok, or Adidas, so long as it kept me from being the butt of the other kids' jokes, especially Luke ,who had a big brother two grades up that everyone feared. This four-foot-nothing kid with an impeccable bowl cut was the ringleader for foot fashion. Luke always and only wore Air Jordans and was quick to point out those who didn't. Unfortunately, my parents didn't have margin for one of these brands and only three days before school I ended up with a pair of high-tops from the local Walmart. I was devastated. More than that, I was fearful of what fate was in store for me as I faced my peers and darkened those school halls on the first day. Everything had led to this point in my young life.

It just so happened that on the Saturday before the start of school, we took my grandmother shopping. We wandered into a second-hand store and there on the shelf I saw them: a white, extra-high-top pair of Adidas tennis shoes. They were two sizes too large for my feet and already had a few scuffs on the soles, but that didn't faze me. They also happened to be the same price as the shoes from Walmart. With my best and most convincing extemporaneous speech, I shared why these would be better shoes for me. My mother allowed the exchange, and a new rush of hope came flooding into my young eight-year-old body.

I showed up to school on Monday ready to take on the world, smile beaming from ear to ear—all was right in the world. And then I heard Luke's voice: "What are you wearing?" As he pointed, the other kids joined in the laughter. "Look at those clown shoes!" Admittedly, they did look like clown shoes. They were far too big, far too tall, far too awkward for my frame. They had the right emblem but they were, in fact, the wrong shoes. In that moment I felt worthless, I felt less than, I felt like a total loser who would undoubtedly drop out of school and most likely life. These shoes, combined with the mockery of my peers, told a story, and it was that this kid wasn't cool. Of course, this is laughable now, and no, the world didn't end that day. But in 1993 at only eight years old, all it took was the opinion of my classmates and a false idea of what life was about to shake my identity to the core. This realization is less laughable and more eye-opening.

A MULTI-FACETED IDENTITY

"What am I?" I bet you haven't asked this question lately, and for good reason. At a base level you are a human. This isn't rocket science, this is how God created you: "So God created man in his own image, in the image of God he created him;

male and female he created them" (Gen. 1:27). After that we start to add certain layers of identification. Step back with me for a minute and let's look at this on three levels: origin, culture, and circumstance. I think this can be a helpful way to see how the concept of identity is not only multi-faceted, but also potentially shaky ground when misunderstood or manipulated.

Origin

"Woman, man, sister, brother, mother, father, son, daughter, so on and so forth." These are all factors of identity that are undeniable and irrefutable. Combined with our humanity, these are, as the Oxford Dictionary would confirm, "The fact of being who or what a person or thing is." The key word here being "fact." Now, although these are our origins, they are all pieces of who we are. This isn't all that I am. In God's creativity He has created each human uniquely. Like a master craftsman, He has taken the time to intricately weave our very being together. "For you created my inmost being; you knit me together in my mother's womb. I praise you because I am fearfully and wonderfully made" (Ps. 139:13-14 NIV). Within our origin identity we are still on solid ground. This level probably doesn't consume your thoughts or add anxiety to your day. It's when we start to move on to cultural identity that we start to feel tension arise.

A DISTORTED IDENTITY

Culture

When you introduce yourself to someone I highly doubt you say, "Hi, I'm Sarah, a human," or, "Hi, I'm Joel, a son." Instead, we are quick to share something about ourselves, usually what we do or who we are connected with. Why do we go here? I was at a small Christian leadership gathering in Seattle several years ago and one of the speakers addressed this very issue. He had spent years researching the culture of the Pacific Northwest and how people connected with one another. He shared that there has been a growing cultural shift in how people greet one another and explained what that is showing us. The leading question time and time again when engaging with a new acquaintance was, "What do you do?" On the surface this may seem harmless but if you look deeper, what's really being asked is, "What is your worth? What do you contribute? Why do you have meaning?" This, combined with an onslaught of social media pressure to be more, do more, have more, and show more, sets the board for a cut-throat game of identity-chess where we often fall prey to false identifiers based on cultural notions.

I recently read an article from a leadership consultant who talked about the growing pressure he would feel when he met new people at conferences. At first he felt the pressure of needing to have a great verbal resume. He would share his title, what he has accomplished, etc. Eventually this became a frustration for him to the point that he realized this was feeding a false sense of identity and he made a conscious effort to stop trying to impress people or prove his worth through accomplishments. Here's what he said happened next.

> And then, at one networking event, I had a moment of clarity. I started introducing myself in this way: "Hi, I'm Simon, I train dolphins to be government assassins." Once again I had attained the level of eyebrow movement that I have attained as a bomb disposal officer (but I guess more out of surprise than respect). Life was easy once again (for a moment at least) but it did make me think. Why do people, including me, care so much about titles? Why would I be prepared to embellish or even make up something about what I do? What does it say about me? The answers to these questions are pretty challenging.[1]

It's not only titles we care about; in the pull of culture we feel a pressure to convince others we are doing enough to justify their time and respect, all the while trying to convince ourselves of the same.

When my close friend Ryan Kearns and I planted Redemption Church in Seattle in 2014, I immediately felt this pressure. I would often work from local coffee shops since we didn't have church offices and were renting a space for services on Sunday. It was a normal occurrence to bump into members of the church family. When asked, "How's your week going?" or, "What are you up to?" I was quick to start verbally vomiting every meeting I had, every task on my plate, every sermon written and it was exhausting. These were people who were not only attending our new church, they were also tithing and making sure that my family was taken care of. I know they didn't mean anything by the questions, but that didn't stop me from trying to convince them I was worthy of their attendance, time, and offerings. It took a solid year, but I came to the realization that I was giving in to identity distortion, and I stopped trying so hard to prove my worth through my efforts (not that I don't still wrestle with this from time to time). It became normal for me to respond to the same questions with very different, genuine answers. "I read a book, I took a long walk and prayed for the church, etc."

"Drew, what in the world does all of this have to do with invisible grief?" Great question! In order to get to the next level that smacks right up against our grief, I need you to see that we enter it with pressure already built. Even without grief, we already find ourselves in the territory of identity distortion, tempted to give in to a completely made-up cultural bar above which we get the title of "successful, valuable, important, impressive," or below it, "useless, a burden, a distraction." Everything in me wants to jump to the end of this chapter and undo the cultural knot that's been tied, but for now I'll do my best to control my ADHD and keep us on track.

Circumstance

In a world marred by the unexpected, where dreams can slip through our fingers like sand and good desires seem to wither on the vine, it's easy to let our pain and losses become the lens through which we see our entire lives. These experiences, while deeply formative, threaten to redefine us if we let them take center stage. We take on new primary names: "barren, single, disabled, orphan, broken, helpless, hopeless." Even though these names are liars (and they definitely are), with chronic grief these false identifiers can grow larger and larger, and become louder and louder. Like a once-beautiful garden left unattended, the weeds start to take over and consume all of the goodness. While this is paradoxical in nature, the longer we sit with and are inundated by a circumstantial identity, whether brought on internally from our view of self or externally by others' view of us, the more comfortable we become with it. "This is who I am." This doesn't happen overnight.

I loved spending summer days with my grandparents as a child in Missouri. On their property was a large red barn. If the St. Louis Cardinals were playing baseball, this is where you would find my grandfather. He would sit with the barn door open, taking in the fresh air and listening to the game on his small silver and black radio, occasionally critiquing along the way but never wavering in his dedication to the team. At seven years old I loved sitting with him for at least a few innings in those worn yellow metal chairs before getting antsy and running to the next thing. Whenever I watch a game, I think back to those summers. I can only imagine what my grandpa Ray would have had to say if he watched game five of the 2014 World Series between the L.A. Dodgers and New York Yankees. Everything seemed to be going right for the Yankees who were up by several runs (five to be exact) midway through the game. But then in the fifth inning the wheels came off. It all started with a routine pop fly that was dropped in the outfield. This eventually led to three more crucial mistakes and five runs scored. It didn't happen all at once, it started slowly and then snowballed. This is the same as many things in life, good, bad, or otherwise: they come about slowly but, if not addressed, have a greater effect than we expected. It's often a slow fade into this kind of false identity, and it points to an uncomfortable truth: What consumes the heart takes on an identity in the mind.

I've watched this play out with friends and parishioners alike, especially in the invisible grief of infertility or unwanted singleness. Cue the questions and suggestions "When are you going to get married?" "When are you going to have children?" "You just need to find a nice guy." "You just need to find the right girl." "Have you tried Christian Mingle?" "Have you thought about adoption?" "You just need to ____." And with this continual reinforcement and the reminder of what isn't, a distorted identity strengthens. This isn't something you asked for and it's definitely not something you wanted, but it also feels heavy and unavoidable like the raincloud that follows Eeyore around in *Winnie the Pooh*.

I want to pause for a moment and speak directly to those who are single and those who don't have children. I want to start by apologizing. The church has historically done a poor job at handling this. We have made assumptions that everyone desires marriage and therefore everyone should be married, but this is not the case! The Apostle Paul, a single missionary, affirms this: "I wish that all of you were as I am. But each of you has your own gift from God; one has this gift, another has that" (1 Cor. 7:7, NIV).

Paul didn't see his singleness as something that made him less than whole, he actually saw it as a gift to be able to minister in the way he was able. If you aren't married and God hasn't given you a desire for marriage, there is nothing wrong with you. You are not less than. If you are married and God hasn't given you a desire for children, don't have children in order to appease the masses who think you should. These are areas in which we need to sit with God and be honest and open. These are not areas we need to feel pressured to pursue for the sake of keeping up with Christian appearances. Shame on us for ever making you feel this way. May we repent and do better in the days to come.

While, at its core, identity is intended to empower us and reassure us of who we are and to what or whom we belong, when distorted through the circumstance of ongoing grief identity can start to have the reverse effect. The negativity that moves from our heart to our mind can make its way into the way we live our very lives. This is where I found myself in 2016 and 2017. Laura and I were walking through infertility and the road was rocky and full of broken glass. It felt impossible not to be consumed by our unmet desire to have children. It was often the first thing on my mind when I woke up and the last thing on my mind as I would fall asleep. As I would look around at those who were experiencing what I longed to experience, it served as a reminder of who I wasn't: a father. The weight of this became heavier and heavier to the point that I began to question whether I should even be a pastor. "What business do I have pastoring people with children if I don't have children?" It was a very real and ongoing thought. It was much more than not being a father, it's what

I started to believe about my identity apart from fatherhood. Not having children now meant I wasn't enough, I was less than, and I wasn't qualified to lead. Looking back, this was ridiculous. It's just as ridiculous as it would be to question the apostle Paul or many of the other disciples for choosing to do the same. Regardless, once this circumstantial identity started to take root, it started to erode truth and my footing became shaky. I was filled with self-doubt, self-hatred, and self-delusion as I allowed infertility to reign over my very worth. Have you felt something similar? Are you there now? You're not alone, and you're also not forgotten.

A RESTORED IDENTITY

Maybe you're familiar with this account. In John 9, Jesus is walking along with his disciples and He encounters a man who was born blind. This is an important part of the story because the disciples automatically make a false assumption about this man's circumstances. "And his disciples asked him, 'Rabbi, who sinned, this man or his parents, that he was born blind?'" (John 9:2). As F.F. Bruce says, "We often suspect that where there is a more than ordinary sufferer, there is a more than ordinary sinner. The disciples believed this so much so that they wondered if this man had actually sinned before he was born, causing his blind condition."[2] The man was blind but he wasn't deaf. He would have already had a very hard life without having to bear the weight of whispers around town as people offered unsolicited judgment on him and his parents. In that time, his blindness meant he would be seen as unclean, which is why he's outside of the temple when Jesus passes by. Most likely, he, like many others in biblical times, would spend his life begging for food, completely dependent on the generosity of strangers and the support of any family they might have. To those around him this man's identity was clear: "blind" meant "burden." Who is this man? He is a blind burden. What a horrible and completely false identity for this societally discarded and forgotten image-bearer of God. Even the disciples buy into this! They aren't the least bit concerned with the man himself, only figuring out why he's blind in the first place. Jesus, though, has other plans.

"Jesus answered, 'It was not that this man sinned, or his parents, but that the works of God might be displayed in him'" (John 9:3). I love this response from Jesus for two reasons. First, He immediately corrects the misguided judgments on behalf of this man. He advocates for him and releases any guilt or shame brought on by the jury of his peers who deemed him or his parents guilty of an act resulting in his inability to see. Jesus makes it abundantly clear: this man is not his blindness. Secondly, He makes it clear that even in this man's pain and loss of sight, God is not done working, not even close. While everyone else may look at this man and see burden and brokenness, Jesus sees belonging and beloved. And with that He offers not only physical healing but so much more. Jesus touches the untouchable and, in doing so, gives him back his dignity and restores his identity.

If you read further in this story you find that this compassionate act on the part of Jesus not only affects the man but his parents too, who stand before the religious leaders and affirm that this is their son—not a burden, not a beggar, their son. Don't forget the main thesis was that his parents had sinned in such a way that they caused their son to be born blind. Imagine being the parents of this man and watching as he not only struggles through life as a beggar on the streets but also has to endure the judgment of others. Why do I think it's important to bring this up? Because for many, invisible grief is felt on behalf of the child they love. In talking with and counseling parents, it is clear that watching a child struggle is one of the hardest things in life. They want so desperately to make everything better. They would do anything to take away the pain.

MEET SCOTT, JANET, AND MADISON

I want to introduce you to two of my friends, Scott and Janet. For the past six years they've attended ONE Fellowship, where I pastor, and recently Scott has joined our staff as director of operations and engagement after retiring from a corporate leadership development career. These are two people you can't help but want to be around. They'll do anything for anyone, and they also have an amazing sense of humor. They're in their late fifties now, but thirty years ago, their world got turned upside down. They were twenty-eight and living in Indiana, and Janet was pregnant with their first child. Everything pointed to a healthy pregnancy and a healthy child. On August 17, 1994 baby Madison was born. This young couple was elated and started this new chapter of parenthood with joy and expectation.

It was Janet who noticed it first. Madison was six months old, and she didn't really respond to loud noises the way other children her age did. She also wasn't making the same noises as other babies make. In place of "babas" and "lalas" were only grunts. At Madison's six-month checkup Janet brought up their concerns. The pediatrician assured her that every child develops at their own pace but, just to be safe, they were referred to an ENT. They decided to administer a general hearing screening that included visual cues and, what do you know, Madison passed. After the first test, the doctors believed her hearing was fine. It was after the second test that the audiologist said, "She knows this test. She's so visual that she was able to memorize the test." They moved to a brain response test. A few months later, now going on a year old, Madison would be put under anesthesia and they would use electrodes to buzz sounds into her head and record the brain's response. As the doctors came to get Madison and take her for this test, they informed Janet that the longer the procedure would take, the better, they start with the loudest possible pitch and work their way down. Janet left to use the restroom and as soon as she came back and sat down, the doctors came out. She knew. Madison was completely deaf.

This wasn't something that ran in either Scott or Janet's families. They were shocked and at the same time inundated with information and the need for further testing to see if this was a byproduct of something else happening in Madison's body. Janet immediately took her daughter upstairs at the hospital to have blood drawn. For one of the tests they needed a urine sample but Madison didn't understand. The nurse started to almost yell at this little girl to give a sample and the grief hit Janet that little Madison didn't follow the directions because she couldn't hear the request. She broke down in the office and started crying. She took home both her daughter, and a new, uninvited reality. As Madison would wrestle with the inability to hear, Janet would wrestle with guilt, and Scott would wrestle with trying to understand why. Why Madison? What would this mean for their daughter, her future, the way she interacted with others, and the way others interacted with her? How would she be seen, identified, stereotyped? One thing was for sure, this long road wasn't going to be an easy one.

A TRUE IDENTITY

In the swirl of our modern existence, where identities are formed and deformed by the relentless pull of culture, success, failures, abilities, inabilities, unmet desires, and shattered dreams, the cry for something more and better and immovable echoes loudly. It's only in the resounding truth of the gospel that we uncover that our deepest identity is not anchored in the frothy waters of cultural bias or circumstance but in the unshakable foundation of Christ. This isn't a Christian bandage for a gaping, lasting wound; this is a master surgeon using precise tools to remove the cancer that's made its way into our heads and hearts.

How and why would the pure and perfect creator reach down and touch the untouchable? Out of love. Out of an unmatched, unwarranted, timeless, and weathered love. God has imputed His righteousness to us through Christ! I know, a nice five-dollar word. But this word is one that carries a weight that, when held, is like kryptonite to the false cultural and circumstantial identities being placed on us. This reality changes everything. As John Piper puts it:

> I know "imputation" is a big and unusual word. But this is the word that has been used for hundreds of years to describe the truth that God "imputes" his righteousness to us through faith because of Christ's obedience. Why should you be denied what tens of thousands of strong Christians have been strengthened by for centuries— the "imputation" of God's righteousness in Christ? It's a glorious truth that will change your life if you see it and savor it for what it is.[3]

This is only possible through a perfect sacrifice and here's what it all means.

> For our sake he made him to be sin who knew no sin, so that in him we might become the righteousness of God (2 Cor. 5:21).

> And because of him you are in Christ Jesus, who became to us wisdom from God, righteousness and sanctification and redemption (1 Cor. 1:30).

Hear these words—please, please hear these words. Because of what Jesus has done on your behalf, when God looks at you, He sees His perfect Son. If you have a relationship with Jesus, being "in Christ" means that your worth, purpose, and belonging are not dictated by the desire that goes unmet, the hope that lingers, or the dreams that have stalled along the way. Rather, these things are centered on the enduring love and grace that define us as His beloved children. Here, amidst shadows and uncertainty, we find the call to rest and flourish in our true identity—an identity that whispers peace, resilience, and wholeness, calling us to a life of profound freedom and purpose. Pain, especially ongoing pain is powerful and loud in the lives of the grieving. We know this; we feel this. But it's here that the darkest night doesn't get the last word, and here that our truest self is not summed up by what we've lost or longed for. Instead, we are drawn into a deeper story where pain is real but not defining, and where our identity is shaped by a love that stands firm through life's fiercest storms. When people are "in Christ," everything changes. The old categories are disrupted. A new identity is revealed, one not bound by past definitions.

Friends, we are the blind man! The glaring difference is we *did* sin and we in turn took on the identity of brokenness and hopelessness. Yet God, in His kindness and grace—through His perfect, blameless Son, took on our worst and gave us His best. We once were blind, but through His grace, oh what a beautiful word, yes grace—we can see! We have, in the greatest sense, been healed and restored. A healing and restoration that doesn't negate our grief, but goes above and beyond it. A healing that will have the final word. As my good friends Justin and Lindsay Holcomb shared in their book, *Rid of My Disgrace,* "To your sense of disgrace, God restores, heals, and re-creates through grace."[4] Our sin once named us; society, circumstance, and even our own flesh have looked to disgrace us; but God has given us a new name, a true identity. "In Christ." In Christ you are not broken, but beloved. In Christ not a sinner, but a saint. In Christ the son or daughter you desperately want to protect and save will never be less than, because Christ is more than enough.

You may feel unseen, unloved, unknown and I'm so sorry for that. I'm sorry for anyone that's added to the pain. I'm sorry for anyone that's spoken lies over you. I'm sorry for those who have said things that have added felt legitimacy to a false identity instead of helping alleviate it. Someone's inability to see your worth doesn't decrease your value. As a pastor, as a friend, as someone who has sat under the weight of identity distortion, this is what I want to shout from the rooftops, until I lose my voice. In Christ, you are seen, known, and loved, without hesitation and without fluctuation. Your name is not single, orphan, infertile, barren, disabled, depressed, bipolar, deaf, lame, blind, chronically ill, or any other form of invisible grief. You have been given a new, unshakable, not-circumstantial name that no one and nothing can take away: beloved son, beloved daughter. As the late, great Brennan Manning says, "Define yourself radically as one beloved by God. This is the true self. Every other identity is illusion."[5]

BACK TO SCOTT, JANET, AND MADISON

Madison came out in the clear for any other medical issues. She was simply a profoundly deaf person. She could feel vibrations but without any hearing. Madison could feel a shotgun blast, but never hear it. She could feel the vibration of a jet engine but without any noise whatsoever. As this young family started down the road on this new journey, hearing aids were the first step. Imagine being a parent and having to hold down your one-year-old daughter who can't grasp what's happening while you struggle to put in these tiny aids that aren't helping at all. After three attempts with three different sets of hearing aids, Madison became eligible for cochlear implants. The waiting list for this newer procedure was years long. As they processed options, they were told that, at best, with sign language and living in a silent world, Madison would max out at a fifth grade reading level. Most likely, this would be their daughter's future.

The weight was heavy and only exacerbated by the fact that Janet was now pregnant with their second child. They decided to move forward with the procedure, uncertain what the results might be but wanting to give their daughter the best opportunity they could. The doctors made it clear: there were absolutely no guarantees on how this would help Madison, or if it would help at all. By God's grace and through "meeting this person who knew this person who put us in contact with this other person," Madison's wait was far shorter than it could have been. After having this invasive surgery—which involved drilling into the mastoid bone behind the ear and implanting electrodes into the cochlea—they had to wait a month to turn the implant on and see what the results would be.

In all of the waiting, Scott and Janet were reminded that Madison, with her infectious personality that would light up a room and those big bows in her hair, was far more than deaf. This was a piece of her life but wouldn't be the whole story, not even close. Easy to say, hard to live out. Yes, they would all have to endure the odd glances, unhelpful remarks, and reality that Madison would have challenges in life that others would not. But they kept moving forward, and God was with them every step of the way. It turns out cochlear implants, newer at the time, were a medical game-changer for the hearing impaired. Madison was able to process much more than the bark of a dog or the sound of a closing door. She blew past that fifth grade reading level, has multiple degrees including a Masters degree in Public Affairs from Indiana University, and has a career with United Way. Just like her parents, Madison has refused to let her deafness define her. Not only that, but she's also been able to encourage and support many others on the same journey. The blind man was ultimately not a blind man; he was a beloved son. Madison is ultimately not a deaf woman; she's a beloved daughter who just happens to be deaf.

HEARING THE TRUTH

No, the header above isn't poking fun at Madison or making light of her inability to hear. (Although, knowing her parents and having met her, I know they would get a laugh out of it.)

At this point we have an important question to ask and answer. How do we embrace and hold on to our true identity in Christ? By hearing the truth over and over again and letting it wash over us. Primarily this happens in three ways: through God's Word, through God's people who affirm God's Word to us, and through the Holy Spirit who continually reminds us of our new and true identity. We'll get to the importance of God's people and community soon, so just for a minute let me unpack the importance of hearing God's Word and listening to the Holy Spirit. If the Bible is our ultimate authority (it is), then taking it in on a daily basis has to be an ultimate priority. There's no way around it. When it comes to believing in and holding on to our true identity in Christ through the journey of invisible grief, God's Word isn't our roadmap. The Word is our bread and the gospel is our water: they sustain us and keep us moving forward. "It is written, 'Man shall not live by bread alone, but by every word that comes from the mouth of God'" (Matt. 4:4).

As we take in God's affirmation about who we truly are, the Holy Spirit takes these truths and applies them to our hearts. As we're about to see in a little while, having this truth applied to us and living in it are critical to walking forward in both joy and grief, as well as to the process of healing. People often use the term "conviction" when they talk about the work of the Holy Spirit. I agree with this when describing the work the Holy Spirit does in the hearts of those who are still far from Jesus. The Apostle John makes it clear, "And when he comes, he will convict the world concerning sin and righteousness and judgment" (16:8). While that is absolutely the role of the Spirit in the world, our judgment, as those who are "in Christ," has been vacated, there is no more conviction. I understand what people mean when they say this, but I also think words are important. If there's any conviction from the Holy Spirit for us, it's the conviction of our righteousness—or a better way to say it, the Holy Spirit reminds us of our true identity, and in doing so points us away from swimming back into the waters of false identity.

There's a vast chasm between grasping this truth in the abstract and weaving it into the everyday fabric of our lives. It's one thing to engage with truth intellectually; it's another to let it permeate our actions and choices until it becomes the pulse that carries us forward. With so many voices speaking, so much noise, it's often that our grief wins our attention by being the loudest. We must take it day by day. We must allow God's grace and the affirming voices of His Word, His people, and His Spirit to remind us of who we really are. This happened for me just a few weeks ago. At the end of a men's conference our church hosted, I was standing in the back to pray for people. One of the other leaders doing the same thing walked over to me. I thought maybe he needed prayer, but then my friend Austin put his arms around me and started praying for me. One line in particular quickly made its way to my heart. "I want to ask that Drew not Drew as a pastor but Drew as your son, would know how loved he is." I needed that, you need that, we all need that. So let's practice it now.

I want to ask you to do something with me. Yes, even as I type this I'm going to do the same. Before you move on to the final words in this chapter, I invite you to lay the book down, take a minute or two of silence, and simply ask God to push aside any distractions and distorted identities and make space for you to hear and receive what He, and only He, says about you. When you've done that, go ahead and take in His truth. I pray that these words become the loudest voice in your life and that they sink deeply into your heart.

GOD SAYS ...

You are the apple of His eye.

Keep me as the apple of your eye; hide me in the shadow of your wing (Ps. 17:8).

You are seen and known.

Before I formed you in the womb I knew you, before you were born I set you apart (Jer. 1:5 NIV).

You are accepted.

Therefore welcome one another as Christ has welcomed you, for the glory of God (Rom. 15:7).

You are loved.

The Lord appeared to us in the past, saying: "I have loved you with an everlasting love; I have drawn you with unfailing kindness" (Jer. 31:3 NIV).

You are secure in His love.

> For I am convinced that neither death nor life, neither angels nor demons, neither the present nor the future, nor any powers, neither height nor depth, nor anything else in all creation, will be able to separate us from the love of God that is in Christ Jesus our Lord (Rom. 8:38-39 NIV).

You are complete in Christ.

> So you also are complete through your union with Christ, who is the head over every ruler and authority (Col. 2:10 NLT).

REFLECTIONS

1. Are there any identity distortions that you have felt or feel the weight of?

2. In our pain, why is holding firm to our true identity in Christ so important?

3. Out of all the statements that God says about you, which resonates with you the most and why?

PURPOSE AND PROMISE

MEET SHELBI

For the past two years I've traveled to London with other pastors and leaders from our church to attend the Leadership Conference hosted by Holy Trinity Brompton (HTB) church. Nicky Gumble and HTB have been transformative in the development of Alpha, a course that helps people engage with some of the biggest questions that surround life and faith. If you aren't familiar, I would recommend checking it out. You never know what to fully expect at this conference; it brings together thousands of people from around the world and from all walks of life and denominations, with Jesus as the unifying thread. What you do know is that there will be amazing speakers and Spirit-filled worship.

It was night two of the conference that we were all introduced to Shelbi Shutt, a young woman with a beaming smile, who was carried in the arms of her husband and placed in a chair at the center of the stage. Over the next thirty minutes, Shelbi would share some of the most impactful words of the entire conference. In high school, life was great for Shelbi. She was also a two-sport varsity athlete. One day during softball practice, while doing sprints with the rest of the team, Shelbi realized she was coming in dead last every time. Something felt off. She went home and told her mom that when she ran it felt like she was carrying 300 lbs of weight on her back—she was completely exhausted. Her mom made an appointment to get her checked out. As Shelbi walked into the doctor's office she gave herself a pep talk: no matter what this is, or whatever they say, you'll be okay and you'll get to the other side of this.

After Shelbi was examined and after tests had been run, the doctor sat down in front of Shelbi and in a very somber tone said, "Shelbi, I'm pretty sure you're showing signs of a very rare neuromuscular disease." Shelbi was shocked and, sure enough, the doctor's educated guess became Shelbi's new reality. She was diagnosed with Limb-Girdle Muscular Dystrophy. This progressive disease deteriorates your muscles over time. When most of us exercise or exert ourselves, our bodies break down muscles, and then re-build them. For Shelbi and those with this rare disease, this isn't the case. The muscle deterioration is permanent. With this type of disease, there is no treatment and there is no cure. Shelbi went back to that pep talk she gave herself and realized there is no other side of this.

Shelbi grew up in the church and had heard incredible stories of healing and how some people had faced hard challenges but put their trust in Jesus and now everything was good. "That's going to be me," Shelbi told herself, time and time again. For the next ten years that belief would take root in Shelbi's life: you encounter something hard, you trust God, and it all ends up okay. When life gets hard, you try harder. And for a while, it felt like that worked. Shelbi married the love of her life, and succeeded in most areas of life. All was going well—until it wasn't. All of a sudden she wasn't doing really well at all of the things that she had managed and controlled. The disease started hitting her body in a totally different way. Shelbi started to feel completely exhausted and was gradually unable to do some of the same things she had previously been able to do.

The turning point for Shelbi was walking into work one day and having a panic attack. It was clear that all of the ways she was trying to manage and control the pain of disappointment in her life weren't working anymore. Shelbi spiraled into a deep pit of depression. At this time she was a student pastor who walked with teenagers who wrestled with anxiety, intrusive thoughts, and suicidal ideations, and now this was true for her. It was overwhelming. Shelbi was at the point of being afraid of what she might do to herself. She wasn't sure she wanted to live anymore. In her most honest prayer she asked God to let her die young. If she had to live life with this progressive disability, she didn't know that she wanted to live. Shelbi ended up checking into an inpatient trauma rehab facility. We'll hear more of Shelbi's story later.

CRUEL GOD OR CRUEL WORLD?

"This was all a part of God's plan." I believe this is one of the most well-intended but totally unhelpful notions offered up to the grieving, especially those with invisible grief. Many don't realize what they're actually saying when these words come rolling off the tongue. We don't stop to consider that brokenness is God's desire. That when God created in Genesis 1, He actually said it was "good." If God needs to bring about bad, in order to accomplish good, there are fundamental issues with the perfect character of God, not to mention our ability to trust Him. So, do we have a cruel God who is bringing pain and grief in order to accomplish His plans, or could it be that we have a broken and cruel world that has gone completely sideways?

The answer to the question above will dramatically shape the way we live with, and think about, both our relationship with God and our grief. Stay with me for a minute while we go back to the beginning in Genesis 1, God creates everything and He declares without hesitation that it is good. What we see, at least for a span of time, is creation living in perfect harmony, exactly as intended. No violence, no pain, no offense, absolutely no brokenness whatsoever. God walking with humanity and humanity walking with God, as the creator intended (Gen. 3:8). All is well, and then the serpent appears. As we talked about briefly before, Satan in the form of the serpent, is able to plant a seed of doubt in Eve's mind. "Did God actually say?" (Gen. 3:1). As Eve processes, Satan offers his own conclusion: "You will not die. For God knows that when you eat of [the tree] your eyes will be opened and you will be like God, knowing good and evil" (Gen. 3:4-5). As Adam and Eve both eat of the fruit, everything changes. "Then the eyes of both were opened, and they knew they were naked" (Gen. 3:7). What once was perfect and good is no more. A life for humanity in perfect communion with God, full of ease and endless joy, now marred by sin that brings pain, sorrow, and doubts into the equation.

The effects were immediate and widespread.

> The LORD God said to the serpent, "Because you have done this, cursed are you above all livestock and above all beasts of the field; on your belly you shall go, and dust you shall eat all the days of your life. I will put enmity between you and the woman, and between your offspring and her offspring; he shall bruise your head, and you shall bruise his heel."
>
> To the woman he said, "I will surely multiply your pain in childbearing; in pain you shall bring forth children.

Your desire shall be contrary to your husband, but he shall rule over you."

And to Adam he said, "Because you have listened to the voice of your wife and have eaten of the tree of which I commanded you, 'You shall not eat of it,' cursed is the ground because of you; in pain you shall eat of it all the days of your life; thorns and thistles it shall bring forth for you; and you shall eat the plants of the field. By the sweat of your face you shall eat bread, till you return to the ground, for out of it you were taken; for you are dust, and to dust you shall return." (Gen. 3:14-19)

God has never been cruel to humanity, quite the opposite. We have been cruel to the creator; we reached for what wasn't ours. Like a bratty child discontent with their meal, we pounded our fork on the table and yelled, "We want more!" We are fully responsible. Humanity ushered in the pain, the brokenness, and, in turn, the grief that would follow. Why would God allow this? God didn't prevent it because to do so would be to force submission in the relationship, and there is no love in that. No, God is not cruel in His allowance of a broken world, filled with broken hopes, broken dreams, broken good desires, but He is absolutely grieved by it. Not a single tear cried, a single knee skinned, or a single love lost was ever a part of His plan, but in His unmatched, long-suffering, perfect love, all is not lost. Wrapped up in the consequences of sin is a promise that will allow goodness and purpose like a bright beam of light to break through the darkness. Did you see it?

I will put enmity between you and the woman, and between your offspring and her offspring; he shall bruise your head, and you shall bruise his heel. (Gen. 3:15)

As soon as things go sideways, God makes it clear that He has a plan to put everything back in order. It won't come through a bolt of lightning, a reset of humanity, or a divine re-ordering of creation, it will come through this unnamed "He." Who is this He that will *crush* the head of Satan, putting death to death once and for all? Jesus. In God's sovereignty, although pain, suffering, and sorrow were never in the plan, He already had a perfect way to bring His kids back home. Cruel God or cruel world? In the words of one of my favorite folk singers Stephen Wilson Jr., "God is good, life is twisted."[1] We ushered in a cruel, broken world, but thank goodness we have a good God who wasn't caught off guard. A God who is able and willing to bring purpose to even our deepest and most drawn-out pain.

PURPOSE IN THE PAIN

In the last chapter, you'll remember we looked at Jesus healing a man born blind in John 9. Jesus' disciples assumed that this man had sinned before birth (not sure how this is possible) or that his disability is the result of his parents' sin. Jesus is quick to correct this false assumption: "Jesus answered, 'It was not that this man sinned, or his parents, but that the works of God might be displayed in him'" (John 9:3). On the surface it might seem that Jesus is saying that God, with intent, caused this man to be born blind. I so appreciate the explanation theologian F.F. Bruce offers here.

> This does not mean that God deliberately caused the child to be born blind in order that, after many years, his glory should be displayed in the removal of the blindness; to think so would again be aspersion on the character of God. It does mean that God overruled the disaster of the child's blindness so that, when the child grew to manhood, he might, by the recovering of his sight, see the glory of God in the face of Christ, and others, seeing the work of God, might turn to the true Light of the World.[2]

God didn't need the man to be blind to accomplish His plans; He didn't need Shelbi to have muscular dystrophy;

He didn't need Aaron to be abandoned by his mother and father; He didn't need Madison to be born deaf; He didn't need Nick to be born without arms or legs, He didn't need Sarah's desire for marriage to go unmet; and He didn't need me and Laura to struggle with infertility. The same is true for whatever you're facing, whatever you're walking with. All of this is true, and at the same time it is equally true that God, in His goodness, won't waste a drop of the pain, the waiting, the grief. As Charles Spurgeon once said, "Cheer up, Christian! Things are not left to chance: no blind fate rules the world. God hath purposes, and those purposes are fulfilled. God hath plans, and those plans are wise, and never can be dislocated."[3] At this point you might be thinking, "Is it just me or has this guy said nothing is wasted a few times now?" Yes, I have! In the invisible grief we carry, we need to hear this truth over and over as we allow it to sink in to the deepest place in our hearts, into the very marrow of our being. God doesn't waste our pain. He redeems it. He uses it. He sanctifies it. To truly believe that God isn't wasting any of our grief, that years of waiting aren't for nothing, that the tears cried haven't gone unseen, we must push back. We must push back on the lie that the pain is purposeless and welcome in the belief that even in the pain there is purpose, more than, dare I say, there is even goodness!

I'd be lying if I said I knew all of the reasons for your grief or how God is using or will use it for good. I don't; no one does. We don't have all of the answers and although it's painstakingly difficult, we need to become okay with that. Spurgeon's words remind me of this, "God is too good to be unkind, and He is too wise to be mistaken. And when we cannot trace His hand, we must trust His heart."[4] I believe there are some foundational purposes that God can bring out of whatever storm we face. I believe this because it is always God's desire to see us grow to be more like Jesus. Here are a few of those, although this list is not exhaustive:

- To grow us in maturity
- To build perseverance
- To grow us in holiness
- To help us uniquely encourage and support others
- To wean us off self-reliance
- To strengthen our assurance in Christ
- To glorify God as we persevere

Could it be that, as my close friend Justin Holcomb shared with me, "God is so sovereign and creative that He can bend brokenness into a tool of blessing?" We see this time after time throughout the Bible. We see this with healing after healing. We see this as Jesus casts out demons. We see this with the infertility of Abraham and Sarah, and Zechariah and Elizabeth. We see this through Moses' speech impediment, through Mephibosheth's inability to walk, through the Apostle Paul's thorn in the flesh that never leaves him. We see this with Joseph and the evil of his brothers; we are reminded of both a broken, cruel world, but also an unthwarted God. Joseph said to his brothers, "As for you, you meant evil against me, but God meant it for good, to bring it about that many people should be kept alive, as they are today" (Gen. 50:20). Time and time again, God doesn't work around the pain and brokenness, but through it.

RETHINKING "GOOD"

But what if we can't see the good? This is a great and important question. There's a big difference between God working in our pain with purpose to accomplish His plans, and us working to make the bad things good as quickly as we can. This can be an incredibly strong pull and one we have to wrestle against. Take Lazarus for example. This was one of Jesus' friends. Not only that, Lazarus was the brother of Mary and Martha whom Jesus loved dearly. I want us to take a look at what Jesus does when He shows up on the scene after Lazarus has died.

> Now when Mary came to where Jesus was and saw him, she fell at his feet, saying to him, "Lord, if you had been here, my brother would not have died." When Jesus saw her weeping, and the Jews who had come with her also weeping, he was deeply moved in his spirit and greatly troubled. And he said, "Where have you laid him?" They said to him, "Lord, come and see." Jesus wept. So the Jews said, "See how he loved him!" But some of them said, "Could not he who opened the eyes of the blind man also have kept this man from dying?" (John 11:32-37)

Do you see it? When Lazarus dies, we observe something profound in Jesus' response. Instead of rushing to try and make it good or fix the situation immediately, Jesus chooses to share in the deep sorrow. He weeps. In each situation He encounters, Jesus invites us to a deeper understanding and a more profound transformation. He calls us to look up, encouraging us to shift our perspectives in ways that often challenge societal norms. Look at these next verses.

> Then Jesus, deeply moved again, came to the tomb. It was a cave, and a stone lay against it. Jesus said, "Take away the stone." Martha, the sister of the dead man, said to him, "Lord, by this time there will be an odor, for he has been dead four days." Jesus said to her, "Did I not tell you that if you believed you would see the glory of God?" So they took away the stone. And Jesus lifted up his eyes and said, "Father, I thank you that you have heard me. I knew

that you always hear me, but I said this on account of the people standing around, that they may believe that you sent me." (John 11:38-42)

Most people would look at this situation and say that the only good thing that could come from this is Lazarus coming back to life. This would be the cultural response. But Jesus makes it clear, that's not what's most important here. Inside of God's plan, the greatest good is not that Lazarus is brought back to life, it's that "the people standing around… may believe that you sent me." We have to be so careful in how we define goodness. If we go with culture's definition, which is essentially "health, wealth, and success," our pain will only increase as our ability to see a good plan from God begins to decrease.

If we believe that Jeremiah 29:11 is true, "For I know the plans I have for you, declares the LORD, plans for welfare and not for evil, to give you a future and a hope" then we need a better definition of what's good. Shelbi helped me see this; she's helping countless others do the same. When I connected with her recently, she articulated this very thing in a way that put words to exactly what I had felt so many years prior and continue to need reminding of these truths today.

> I believe all pain, all suffering is an invitation to see with greater clarity that which will remain and that which will not. In this God is reorienting our hearts to what good actually is. When we can't see the good, we grieve knowing that God grieves with us, and we allow it to increase our hunger for His return. When we allow that future hope to be pulled into the foreground of our current reality, no matter what we face or walk through, we are bathing in the goodness of God.

Are we okay if God's plan for good in our lives looks different than our idea of good? Are we okay if His plan is different than ours? This isn't a hypothetical question; it's something we need to sit with, pray through, and wrestle with. If we are willing to engage on this level, God will meet us there just as He promised in His Word, "Trust in the Lord with all your heart and lean not on your own understanding; in all your ways submit to him, and he will make your paths straight" (Prov. 3:5-6).

BACK TO SHELBI

Nothing has changed physically for Shelbi, and yet everything has changed for Shelbi emotionally and spiritually since she checked into that inpatient facility, especially when it comes to the way she sees her pain, God's purpose, and His plan for her life. On that night in London, Shelbi shared a powerful message on the sufficiency of God's grace, no matter the pain or the circumstance. I connected with Shelbi a few months ago. We talked about grief, purpose, honesty, and where this intersects with Jesus. Instead of me speaking for her at this point in her story, I'll let her speak directly.

> I had spent so much of my life trying to bypass my way around the pain of living life with a disability. When I came honestly before God with the truth of what was really going on, He was there. Where I was focused on a day that I would enter into where there is no pain and no more sorrow, I found it was Jesus redefining that the Kingdom is here and now and it's in and with me—that totally shifted my perspective. It's being with Him, it's doing life with Him, it's receiving His love and loving Him in return. I can be loved in the midst of my desperate need and deep longings, because He meets me there.

To properly see our grief along with God's plans and purpose with twenty-twenty vision, we have to come to the realization that God's ultimate purpose for you and me is the same as it is for anyone else, regardless of what we are or aren't facing. This isn't diminishing or downplaying our pain, it's shining a bright and proper light on God's ultimate purpose and plan for our lives.

In the truest and greatest sense we are called to live in the reality of who God says we are and advance His kingdom as we love Him, love others, and point anyone and everyone to Jesus while also pursuing Him ourselves. This is our purpose, while grieving and rejoicing, on the mountain and in the valley. This brings our creator glory! This is true for the brother and sister in the United States just as it's true for the brother and sister in Uganda. This is God's ultimate kingdom purpose for His children. When we are able to press in to this reality, it allows us to not only see more clearly, but also to hold on to His promise as we look ahead more fully.

PROMISE THROUGH THE PAIN

> And we know that in all things God works for the good of those who love him, who have been called according to his purpose (Rom. 8:28).

There is only one way that we can stare our grief in the mirror and at the same time speak these words with confidence. This is something Joni Eareckson Tada has had to do for most of her life. At the age of seventeen she experienced a life-altering diving accident that left her a quadriplegic. She has dedicated her life to sharing her faith and empowering others. Along with being an author and renowned speaker, she is also a fierce advocate for those with disabilities. Even in the pain and loss, even in the unknown, Joni loves to share this encouragement: "When I am distressed, when pain seems overwhelming, when I feel I cannot go on, I hold fast to God's promises. They keep my mind from wandering down dark, depressing paths."[5]

Here's what I find most difficult about promises, even promises from God that I also believe, like Joni, will endure. First, we live in a world where promises are broken every day. For some, we've witnessed broken promises wreaking devastation and heartache across relationships, rippling through entire families. People have walked away when they said they wouldn't. Parents walked out when you needed them most. A spouse sits you down to tell you it's just too hard and they've fallen out of love. It is no surprise to any of us that we live in a culture of contracts, not covenants. Like the stray dog that came and visited my house when I was ten, we are hesitant to trust and are easily skittish.

Secondly, if you are living with unreconciled, invisible grief, you are living the in-between. That is to say, you are living in the gap between God's promises of good plans and seeing them come to complete fruition. The in-between, the already but yet to come, is hard. It's painfully difficult at times. It can be hard to read Jeremiah 29:11, "For I know the plans I have for you," declares the LORD, "plans to prosper you and not to harm you, plans to give you hope and a future," and not think, "Good for them, sure, but probably not me. A hope and a future for them, but just more pain waiting for me."

Knowing our potential hesitation when it comes to promises for a good future, I'm reminded of what Jeremiah has to say a few chapters later, chapter 33. I just preached on this passage a few weeks ago and I often find myself going back to it. If you aren't familiar, this is an incredibly dark time for God's people. In the darkness, we tend to get lost or start running in the wrong direction, and this is no different.

In the historical context of this passage in Jeremiah, God has made past promises but the people have decided to go their own way. The year is 587 B.C. and the king of Babylon and his troops have surrounded the capital city of Jerusalem, setting up a deadly siege and leaving the people inside Jerusalem on the brink of starvation. This is only the beginning. Countless lives will be lost and God's people will be exiled from the home they once knew. Jeremiah himself is sitting in a cold prison when God shares these words with His faithful prophet.

> Behold, the days are coming, declares the LORD, when I will fulfill the promise I made to the house of Israel and the house of Judah. (Jer. 33:14)

In the midst of the darkness of a war-torn people, when all seems utterly hopeless, Jeremiah shares these words. Okay, so when? How long, O Lord? Herein lies the crux. The only thing lacking in God's promises isn't the assurance of what's coming, it's the timetable for when it's coming and what exactly the "good" will be.

I believe that holding on to promises for our good and envisioning a joyful future, in the middle of pain can be among the most challenging parts of our life and our faith. This requires hope, and hope means vulnerability. Like Kryptonite to Superman, this is how vulnerability can feel to the grieving. We shudder at the thought of opening ourselves up for fear of further disappointment. Vulnerability can feel like having a secondary heart surgery while we're still trying to recover from the first: uncomfortable and complicated. I appreciate what Craig Groeschel says about this idea, "There is pain in the moment, and hope for the future. But sometimes the pain seems to yell, while hope only whispers."[6]

To hope is to look forward to the future with expectation. I don't know about you, but expectation can feel risky in general, not to mention when you're walking through a long season of grief that's birthed out of the "here and not yet." In the words of one of my favorite movie characters, Red, from one of my favorite movies, *The Shawshank Redemption*, "Hope is a dangerous thing. Hope can drive a man insane."[7] What do we do when we find ourselves at this crossroad? We can take the first path, which is familiar and comfortable. It's somewhat cold, and it's dark, but it's known. With little room for risk, this path takes us back and forth from where we've been and where we will be with little change. But there's another other path. This second way is less known, and it requires us to plant our feet in places we aren't used to. We see a glimmer of light but it's hard to make out. At times we can barely see the hand in front of our face, but even in the dark, even when we hesitate, all the while, we hear these warm words from a faithful friend who walks with us, reassuring us as we put one foot in front of the other.

> Do not fear, for I am with you;
> do not be afraid, for I am your God.
> I will strengthen you; I will help you;
> I will hold on to you with my righteous right hand
> (Isa. 41:10 CSB).

I want to invite you to consider taking the second path. If you're like me, you've spent far too much time on the familiar, cold path of safeguarding, not realizing that the best path, the truly good path, the safest path, is actually the second. Yes, there is faith required, there is a necessity of trust, and there is an unclenching of fists that must take place, but all the while we are with the one who created the path. He knows it like the back of His hand, and He holds our hand in His as we take each step. I want us to start this journey not haphazardly but with a question and a call that go hand in hand.

A QUESTION OF TRUST

We started this chapter looking at pain and purpose in the midst of our grief. I see promise as the divine glue that holds all of this together. I believe it's easy to overcomplicate these concepts so, in an attempt to do the opposite here, here is what lies between God's promise for your good and your belief in that promise. What it comes down to is a question, a question that carries the weight of our very lives, the weight of our pain, and the possibility of purpose in all of it. It is a question I come back to regularly, especially when pain is yelling and hope only seems to whisper. It's the question that reframes and reorders my greatest doubts and often quiets my restless heart. Here it is: Can I trust the one making the promise? As I lay in bed at night surrounded by deafening silence, do I trust that God actually has good in store for me? As I go through another day where I watch others live out my hopes and dreams, do I trust that God hasn't forgotten about me or misplaced His plans for my life? As I close out another day and feel defeated, do I trust that He is able to renew my joy?

There can be this false idea that Christianity is about having this blind, close your eyes and cross your fingers kind of trust. This couldn't be further from the truth, and this way of thinking is dangerous at best. Faith, in and of itself, is worthless. Tim Keller makes this clear when he writes, "strong faith in a weak branch is fatally inferior to weak faith in a strong branch."[8] It's where our faith is placed that gives it value and worth, even when that faith has grown thin. Trust in God is never pulled out of thin air. It's based on a history with God, a history that gives us glimpses of His character and shows why we should place our trust in Him. It's never based on our wishful thinking or positive feelings. Is faith required? Absolutely. But not blind faith. The required faith is a faith that stands on a history of good purposes and good plans, even for imperfect people.

By faith Noah trusted God and built an ark, saving his family. By faith, Abraham and Sarah received the son God promised them, even though they were too old to bear children. By faith, Joseph overcame betrayal, slavery, false accusations, and imprisonment to save the nation of Israel. By faith, God's people left Egypt and walked through the Red Sea as it parted on each side for them. By faith, the Israelites marched around the walls of Jericho, and the walls came tumbling down. The list goes on and on. These weren't perfect people. They all had struggles, doubts, mistakes, flaws, and weaknesses, but they all had one thing in common: they put their hope in God and persevered in faith, waiting on God to show that He keeps His promises, and that He's trustworthy again and again. As Philip Yancey says, "Faith means believing in advance what will only make sense in reverse." I believe God has a perfect track record of keeping His promises, a record that goes all the way back to Genesis and stretches all the way into your life today, no matter what you are walking through or how dark the path has become.

Can I trust the one making the promise? In our invisible grief, like a song stuck on repeat, we are constantly being reminded of what hasn't been and what may never be. With this reminder comes the temptation to answer this question in the negative. This is why the call to remember is so important. Remember the goodness of God. His promises kept in the past are an open invitation to believe in His goodness and trust His promises into the future.

A CALL TO REMEMBER

We are a forgetful people. The older I get and the more inundated I become with life's complexities, anxieties, distractions, and otherwise, the easier I find it to forget. It is a regular occurrence that I walk into a room in my house and just as soon forget why I'm even there (unless it's the kitchen, I always know why I'm there). In the swirl of pain that can be so confusing at times, we have to remember. We desperately need to remember. This was true for God's people of old and it's just as true for you and me. We have to look back and see how God has shown up time and time again. We are a people of remembrance. Every week in our church we practice this through communion as we come and remember what Christ has done for us, what we could never have done for ourselves. In the same way, it's remembering God's goodness and His kept promises that helps keep us from forgetting and, like sheep without a shepherd, wandering into utter despair and the false belief that our pain is meaningless or that we've been left to fend for ourselves. Remembering God's goodness is like pouring gas on the altar of hope, and this hope won't be put to shame (Rom. 5:5).

Let me pose three questions for you to sit with and actually answer. I've found these personally beneficial over the years, especially when doubt or skepticism creeps in. How has God been faithful and good in my personal history with Him? (Think small, think large, include it all.) How has God been faithful and good in the lives of people around me? How has God been faithful and good among His people throughout the history of His Word?

Sometimes "good" needs re-defining according to God's will, not culture's way—as Shelbi spoke to earlier—and sometimes we simply have to come open-handed with faith like a child, trusting that even though our hands are empty, somehow, someway, God is going to fill them. At other times we have to accept that the good God has promised, and all of the unique forms it might take in our life, is beyond our understanding. This isn't a cop-out; this is actually a sign of growth, of maturing in our faith. It's okay to admit we don't have all of the answers. This is often one of the healthiest confessions we can make, because it's true. We don't have the control our flesh fights for, and we don't have all of the answers our weary heart longs for, but do we trust the one making the promise? I've wrestled with this question more times than I can count. I'm guessing in some form or fashion you have too. It's kept me up at night, it's held me captive time and time again. For me and Laura this became a constant wrestling match. Not only were we struggling with trust, but we were also paralyzed by the idea of taking the wrong steps if we did move forward. But somewhere along the way, over time, God's promises started to soften us. He started to remind us that His promise of "I have good" could just as easily be translated into "I haven't forgotten you." Were things broken? Yes. Was the pain of infertility real? Yes. But in the midst of it all was God growing us, stretching us, and solidifying our faith? Was God assuring us that none of this waiting would be wasted, that there would be purpose unmistakable, and good plans immeasurable, whether in this life or the one to come? Yes.

THE SECOND PATH

After countless hours processing with each other, and with friends and family, and after relentless prayer, even as faith seemed thin at times and trust still teetered, we believed God had a hope and future for us. We didn't want to just jump into something because it made sense on paper. We weren't looking for a "Plan B" or a quick fix even though countless well-intended people had offered up wonderful unsolicited advice like, "you should just adopt" as if we were deciding what to order from a takeout menu. We were scared; there were unknowns, and plenty of fears. Ultimately what it came down to was the belief that God had placed a good desire within both of us to expand our family, whatever that would look like and in whatever timing. In late 2016 we began the adoption process. I have two adopted cousins and have witnessed firsthand the beauty of adoption. This is at the very heart of God. I believe it's quite possibly the most gospel-centered reflection that can be witnessed on this earth. It is a small glimpse into the sprawling landscape of God's love for us, His children that He's adopted into His family and and to whom He has given a lasting inheritance. Full family rights, a permanent place at the dinner table! Those who were once orphaned by sin have found a home filled with love and care along with an ever-expanding family that now carries Jesus' DNA. It doesn't get better than this.

I want to make something clear: we were still carrying the weight of grief, but we also started to realize that it's absolutely possible to carry grief and joy simultaneously. The next chapter is all about this. Over the next six months we filled out piles of paperwork, went to training, listened to audiobooks, completed our home study with Kyla our adoption coordinator, and made a book to share with prospective birthparents, and then we waited. It would not be an easy wait. It would be two years filled with hills and deep, deep valleys. But we stayed on the second path, gripping the hand of one who held our hands tightly, and we stepped forward one small step at a time, listening closely as we heard:

Do not fear, for I am with you;
do not be afraid, for I am your God.

I will strengthen you; I will help you;
I will hold on to you with my righteous right hand.
(Isa. 41:10 CSB)

On January 8, 2019 I celebrated my thirty-fifth birthday. Celebrate is a stretch. Any milestone like birthdays, Mother's Day, or Father's Day, just felt like cruel reminders of what wasn't. I'll be honest, I don't remember anything about this birthday. You can ask Laura: I would transform into Scrooge anytime my birthday would roll around. On my thirtieth, Laura wanted to throw me a party and instead I convinced her to eat pizza with me alone on the couch and watch *Good Will Hunting*. (It was fantastic!) So no, I don't remember January 8, 2019. I can't tell you what I did, what I ate, any of it, but I'll never forget what happened on the 10th.

It was a Thursday, and I was working from home. Laura was a teacher at a Christian school in Seattle and left for work around 7:30 a.m. I don't know why, but I remember being in an unusually bad mood that day. I think it was the birthday emotional hangover from two days before that led me back to bed that morning. I just didn't have much to give. Then at 10:10 a.m. my phone starting ringing. I looked at the ID and it was Kyla, our adoption counselor. Even writing this transports me back to that hundred-year-old home on NE 56th Street. I can feel the original hardwood flooring under my feet and I can smell the candles covering the must of the old home. Kyla said that there was a birthmother in South Carolina who went online and saw our profile (this never happens). And then these words that felt like God Himself was speaking them: "She wants you and Laura to be the parents of her son." It's impossible to describe on paper that moment and the moments that followed, but it felt like my heart exploded in the best way. In that moment fear lost its footing and hope took the next dance. The words "For I know the plans I have for you, declares the LORD, plans for welfare and not for evil, to give you a future and a hope" rang as loud as Christmas bells from an old church cathedral.

I didn't know what to do but I knew it was a time to celebrate. If there was ever a time to celebrate it was now! I called my good friend Alex, with whom I was pastoring at the time. He came over quickly, most likely concerned at the level of energy I exuded over the phone. I told him I was going to be a dad, and we cried together in my kitchen. Dad: forever my favorite name. After he left I didn't know what to do, but I soon found myself at a local Target buying baby formula and wiping away tears as I slowly walked down each aisle, imagining what our son would look like and dreaming about my family's future. A future filled with hope. Something that felt so distant for so long, something so foreign, finally started to take shape. It wasn't what I expected seven years prior, it wasn't what we prayed for day after day and night after night, but somehow, in God's love, in His goodness, in His sovereignty and perfect plans, I knew it was better. Romans 8:28 went from cold black letters on a page, to a vibrant explosion of lights and sounds. You remember?

> And we know that in all things God works for the good of those who love him, who have been called according to his purpose (Rom.8:28 NIV).

I was able to embrace the first part of the verse for the first time. *God works.* Like a stage manager working in the shadows, pulling levers and making moves that go unseen, God had never stopped working even when I stopped hoping. He never put it into cruise control even when I questioned His care. Yes, He was working around me, He was working in me, He was orchestrating a beautiful symphony using broken instruments and trash can lids for drums. Take heart my friend, He is still working.

On January 28, 2019 Silas Jaxon Hensley was born. In case we needed more affirmation on God's plans, Kyla reached out to us a week after the initial call to ask if we had chosen a name. When we shared that we had decided on Silas (not the most common name) she was speechless as she told us that our son's birthmother had chosen the same name during her first few months of pregnancy. As soon as we set eyes on this little 6 lb, 7 oz bundle of joy, our hearts were filled. For the first time in seven years God gave us a greater glimpse of kindness than we had ever experienced. This was never Plan B; in God's sovereign ability, even in our brokenness, this was His Plan A. I believe with every fiber of my being that Silas was always intended to be my son. God didn't need us to be infertile to get there but that was the path it took. I can't tell you how it all works, I just trust that God is big enough and good enough to create a beautiful garden where there was once only desert.

> No less God within the shadows
> No less faithful when the night leads me astray
> 'Cause You're the heaven where my heart is
> In the highlands and the heartache all the same.[9]

WHAT ABOUT ME?

At this point you might be thinking, "That's great for you, Drew, but what about me?" What about those of us who walk through our entire lives without the hope, dream, or good desire coming to life? This is a fair question. As we're going to talk about a little later, even with the adoption of our son, our grief over our infertility didn't magically go away. It's a grief we carry and will carry for the rest of our lives in some form, even though God has met us in the grief and has shown His kindness and goodness. It doesn't define us, but it is a part of our story within God's greater story.

Look, I don't know you, but I know you picked up this book or were handed this book or downloaded this book. Whoever and wherever you might be, without hesitation I pray that God fulfills your hopes, dreams, and good desires. I believe that our God is able. I believe that the God we love is able to heal in ways that surpass understanding. I believe He is a miracle worker who is not bound to human limitations. I've anointed countless heads with oil, praying prayers of supplication on others' behalf and believing that if God so chose He could make the sick well, remove the mental illness, make the lame able to walk, bring conception for the infertile, and provide spouses, all in that very instant. And so like you, I pray and I plead that He brings the spouse, brings the children, cures the illness, restores the relationships, makes bright the future and brings absolute healing in a way that can only be credited to Adonai (Lord Master), El Gibhor (The Mighty God), El Roi (The God Who Sees), Immanuel (God With Us), Jehovah-Jireh (The Lord Our Provider), Jehovah Rohi (The Lord Our Shepherd).[10] As I write this, I'm praying this. Keep praying, keep pleading, keep knocking on God's door in the middle of the night.

And if He answers in the way your heart desires, fall at your knees in worship. With childlike awe, allow the words from Psalm 115 to flow from your mouth and be the resting place of your heart, "Not to us, O Lord, not to us, but to your name give glory, for the sake of your steadfast love and your faithfulness!...The Lord has remembered us; he will bless us" (vv 1, 12).

An even if God doesn't, still fall at your knees and worship knowing that He has good plans. Take confidence that He already knows your future, as He is not bound by time. The very God who promises to go with you through peaks and valleys also promises to go before you. I love these words from Deuteronomy 31:8, a promise worth holding on to and taking heart in:

> The Lord himself goes before you and will be with you; he will never leave you nor forsake you. Do not be afraid; do not be discouraged (Deut. 31:8 niv).

As my good friend Isaac, a friend well-aquainted with invisible grief, says and has framed in his home, "And if not, He is still good." Even to not have all of the answers and to not know all of the future, even to not see all of the pieces line up as we hoped they would, He is still good and He has good for you. You are His child whom He loves more than anything. Here's how I know.

A CALL TO THE CROSS, A CALL TO INTIMACY

The greatest promise God has ever made comes through Jesus. All of God's promises are made good through Jesus. As John Piper says, "Before the promises of God can have much savor to us, Jesus Christ, the seed of Abraham and the great hope of all nations, has come. In Him, all the promises of God find their Yes and Amen."[11] The promise birthed from the pain in Genesis 3 stretches all of the way to here, now, and beyond. A promise fulfilled as a humble king moves from cradle to cross. It's not enough to just remember what God has done in and around us; we must go sit at the cross time and time again, making a second home there as we remember what God has done for us; the grace that He has shown us. When it feels like you've been forgotten and God has gone silent, when His idea of goodness doesn't feel that good, we have to go sit at the cross and remember. In the poetic words of minister and author Matthew Henry, "Come, and see the victories of the cross. Christ's wounds are your healings, His agonies your repose, His conflicts your conquests, His groans your songs, His pains your ease, His shame your glory, His death your life, His sufferings your salvation."[12] Doubts will come, other voices will speak, but the cross speaks the loudest. In His death and resurrection, the battle cry comes: All is not lost, hope has come! In all of the pain there is purpose, and a secure promise.

> For I am convinced that neither death nor life, neither angels nor demons, neither the present nor the future, nor any powers, neither height nor depth, nor anything else in all creation, will be able to separate us from the love of God that is in Christ Jesus our Lord (Rom. 8:38-39 NIV).

Embrace this truth with the same tender ferocity. God enfolds you in His everlasting arms. Let it seep into the cracks of your heart, inscribed there by the gentle yet incisive hand of the one we call Abba. He hasn't called us to do, He's called us to be. He has called us to intimacy with Him, a Father who knows us and a big Brother who loves us. No matter the circumstance, no matter the grief, no matter how God chooses to move in your life from this day forward, this is the ultimate answer to Romans 8:28 and how all things will work together for our good: it's Jesus! Every dream, desire, and hope finds it rightful place under the beautiful, incomparable, beating heart of the gospel. This is the paradoxical nature of God's goodness. It makes absolutely no sense on paper. Why move into our mess? Why offer a perfect Son for prideful liars and thieves? How in the world can this be good? Here's how:

> Jesus, the founder and perfecter of our faith, who for the joy that was set before him endured the cross, despising the shame, and is seated at the right hand of the throne of God (Heb. 12:2).

In the shadows of Gethsemane, we witness that Jesus did not seek the torment of the cross. He didn't hope for the pain that would await. His heart laid bare in the garden, where He pleaded with His Abba, "Father, if you are willing, remove this cup from me. Nevertheless, not my will, but yours, be done" (Luke 22:42). With a seemingly reckless trust, born out of unfathomable love, He submitted to the Father's will—not for obedient disciples but for the unruly, the ungrateful, the wayward children who go kicking and screaming. He didn't run, He didn't go numb, He didn't question His father's care, He saw beyond.

In the heart of it all, Jesus was journeying back to the Father—an unspeakable homecoming just on the horizon. Yet, in that unfathomable economy of grace and sacrifice, He wasn't making the journey alone. Through the mystery of His suffering and the stark embrace of the cross, He crafted a path from pain to promise and invited us to follow, each of us cradled in the shadow of His sacrifice.

There's something almost absurdly beautiful in the idea that through that loss, He's leading us, one by one, back from shattered dreams and fractured lives, drawing us ever closer to the sacred warmth of home. So there we are, carried—each with our own stories of brokenness—guided on a journey that, in ways unimaginable, promises that we are not only seen and known, but we are loved beyond all measure. He is leading us back home. We'll talk more about this final promise as we get closer to the end of our conversation.

I want to end this section by leaving you with a few lyrics that have been meaningful to me lately, a song that continues to resonate. A call to remember, a call to surrender. Before you move to the next chapter, take a few minutes for silence and solitude. Sit and remember.

When my heart is racing deep inside my chest
When I'm underneath the weight of anxiousness

When my fear is raging and I can't catch my breath
I will remember

You are faithful still
You have carried me through deeper waters
Walked beside me through the fire
Gone before me and You always will
You are faithful still

God, You saw this long before I knew
And Your peace is waiting here to see me through
My deliverance is only found in You
So I will surrender

You are faithful still
You have carried me through deeper waters
Walked beside me through the fire
Gone before me and You always will
You are faithful still[13]

REFLECTIONS

1. Why is it so important that we have a good understanding of where brokenness comes from? What is the danger if we don't?

2. What stands out in the account of the man born blind from John 9?

3. Why are God's promises and the call to remember so important as we walk through a long season or life of grief? What promises are you holding on to tightly? Which ones do you still wrestle with?

4. In your own words, why do we need to go back to the cross again and again?

A LETTER TO SILAS

DEAR SILAS,

I know that one day you'll read this book, or at least skim through it. What I hope you see the clearest is that God is so good and that He loves His kids, even when life is hard and doesn't go the way we expect. Your mom and I have been learning this more and more over the years. It hasn't always been easy, but God has always been working, even when we couldn't see it. We so badly wanted to have you as our son. We prayed and prayed for you. So many people prayed for you. We thought that this would happen biologically, but God had other plans. There is nothing that could keep us from you. Even in our pain and when we didn't know what our family would look like, God always knew. He's just that powerful and just that good. He knew we had been alone without you long enough. You are the greatest gift that God has given us on this earth. You have filled our hearts in ways we didn't even know were possible. When I look at you, son, I see the kindness of Jesus every single day, and that's an amazing, priceless gift.

You are so loved. When I watch your mom hug you I see her heart get three sizes bigger, just like in the *Grinch* movie you love so much. It doesn't matter where we are, whenever you run up and give me one of your amazing hugs it feels like home. Son, you are more loved than you will ever fully know or grasp, and you are most loved by God. He made all of this possible. He made you, every single part of you! He loves us so much and He's always taking care of us.

I love you, buddy, and I can't imagine a day without you in it!

With so much love,
Dad

PART 3

HOW WE MOVE FORWARD

8

IN GOSPEL COMMUNITY

It was Saturday morning. The gray clouds outside of our quiet Seattle home matched how Laura and I both felt. We got our hopes up from being told that our profile was one of only two being shown to a birth mom, only to be met with the familiar disappointment a day later when we received the news that she chose the other family. This had happened a few times. You might think we would have been used to it or more emotionally prepared, but not at all; each time it felt like a new wound being opened. All of the emotions came flooding in, all of the doubts, all of the anger, all of the loud internal voices saying "less than" and "broken." This emotional and mental exhaustion quickly turned to physical exhaustion. We didn't want to see anyone. We didn't expect to see anyone. We only shared this news with a select few people and planned on immersing ourselves in Netflix for the next twelve hours. It was 9 a.m. when we heard a knock at the door. "Oh goodness," I thought, "who is it and how quickly can we get them to leave?" As Laura opened the door I could hear the voice before I saw the face. It was Katie. Katie and Ben were two of our closest friends, and still are. They had walked with us every step of the way once we finally opened up about our grief. Today wouldn't be any exception. Katie was welcomed in, partially because she brought a dozen donuts from Top Pot, irrefutably the best donut shop in Seattle (sorry Mighty-O). If you know me, I'm not one to turn down a good donut. She informed us that Ben had their four girls for the day and she would be here with us doing a whole lot of nothing.

As I think back on that day, I'm reminded that Katie didn't come over and try to fix anything or even cheer us up. She just came to be present, to sit with us in the heartache, to care for us and dress our wounds with kindness. She was a true gutter buddy. No, that's not an insult, it's a compliment. Some people are quick to try to pull you out of the gutter, but it's the friends who are willing to jump down with you and sit as long as it takes who make all the difference to the grieving heart. It's an ongoing reminder not that everything is okay, but that you aren't alone. We all need Ben and Katies in our life. We all need Justins, Ryans, Bryce and Janas. We need Alex and Jeremys, Lauren and Jonathans. We need community. More than that, we need gospel-community. This isn't to say that those who don't share our faith can't be an important part of community support, but that those who do need to stand at the forefront. We need community in the good, in the bad, and when it feels like the wheels have come off completely. We need people who, when grief that's going to stick around gets dropped in our laps, are going to stick around as well and for as long as it takes.

CREATED FOR COMMUNITY

Have you been to a middle-school dance lately? Boys on one side of the room, girls on the other. You can cut the awkwardness with a knife. And then, that one brave boy or girl (let's be honest, it's probably a brave girl) crosses the room and asks for a dance. As hormones rage and palms sweat one thing is clear: this is so much better than standing alone against that cold wall. The gospel whispers of a love that invites us into a dance not meant for one, but for the gathered. From the dawn of the sacred text, when the creator gazes upon Adam and declares, "It is not good that man should be alone" (Gen. 2:18), a divine promise unfurls: you are called into community. Community, a beautiful reflection of God Himself, is the very essence of what it means to walk together, with the Father, Son, and Spirit.

Think about the formation of Israel. This was never just about a solitary soul, but about a people fashioned to reflect the relentless tenderness of God. His commandments knit a tapestry of justice, compassion, and shared life among His beloved.

And then, in the luminous grace of the New Testament, Jesus steps onto the scene to tell us that love looks like neighbors (Luke 10:27), like outstretched hands, like unity in the mess of life. We move forward and we see that the fledgling church depicted in Acts is not simply a collection of individuals but a family sharing bread, resources, hearts— the very essence of grace embodied (Acts 2:42-47).

Need more proof that you were made for community? In the Apostle Paul's letters, those profound sighs of love and longing spoke to whole communities, urging them to bear each other's burdens, to grow together as an interconnected body of grace. We are not isolated wayfarers; we are part of a sacred body, drawn together by divine love.

The call of the gospel is not to go it alone but to embrace the messy, beautiful truth of community, intertwined with the one who loves you beyond reason. Our wounds are not meant to heal in isolation but in the embrace of one another—a band of misfits loved fully by God and called to love just the same.

GOSPEL COMMUNITY IS MESSY

Yes, you are made for community, but in your grief you will be tempted to hide from community—or at least hide your pain and loss from community. Whether that's the community of a friend, a few friends, or an entire group. Laura and I have found both to be true. Community is messy. It's not a place where everyone will have all of the right answers (whatever that means) or say all of the right things. It is, as we are, fatally flawed and yet a divine gift in seasons of joy, sorrow, and mundanity. While there are a variety of reasons why we are tempted to pull back and keep to ourselves like small children taking their toys and hiding them away, here are a few I believe are prevalent as I've talked with others and have closely observed this temptation in my own life.

We Are a Mess

When I was ten, a stray dog made its way to the front porch of my house. I didn't have a dog, but I really wanted one, so this would be that dog—or so I thought. The dog was small and had cuts and scars, it's hair was tangled and you could tell it had been through something. Out of what I believe was pity for their ten-year-old son, my parents allowed me to feed the dog, but didn't let me bring it inside our home. Even at ten I could tell the animal was scared and hesitant to trust me. Slowly but surely it made its way to the food and water bowls and began to eat. I remember reaching over to pet the dog (huge mistake, don't pet any animal while it's eating). At first the dog didn't seem to mind the touch of my hands gently petting its head. And then it happened: out of nowhere the dog bit me.

You've probably heard it said that hurt people hurt people. While this may sound like a simple one liner, I've found it to be consistently true. As the walking wounded it is easy, and sometime often, that we go into the mode of protection or projection. We pull away from people or we push back on people's kindness, all for the sake of protecting ourselves. We also project our pain onto others. When wounds don't begin to scar and they stay open for an extended period of time, the pain has to go somewhere. This was a part of me for years. I had a short fuse with Laura and others, not because I wanted to hurt them but because I myself was hurting and this was an outlet. At times I found myself having unrealistic expectations that I would place on people around me, and I often would greet kindness with hurtful words. Thank goodness for the grace to be able to go and ask for forgiveness and receive it. Yes, like that stray dog, in our pain and loss, we tend to bite.

We Are Overwhelmed and Tired

> Be gracious to me, O LORD, for I am languishing; heal me, O LORD, for my bones are troubled (Ps. 6:2).

Grief, especially ongoing grief, can wreak havoc on our bodies. We see this in Scripture. David makes it clear that the pain he feels, the loss of relationship he feels as he's on the run, are manifesting physically. According to a UCLA study, grief can bring a lowered immune system, insomnia, and mental and physical fatigue, just to name a few. Throughout our darkest seasons of grief Laura and I hosted a community group. I deeply loved these people, but I cannot tell you how many nights I wanted nothing to do with the gathering. I was tired and mentally worn out, sometimes depressed, sometimes anxious. At times, the idea of being with others simply feels overwhelming. The point here is not, "Just do it! Who cares that you're tired." The point is not to allow this to become the norm. The days we feel tired and worn may be some of the days we need to be with other people the most.

We Don't Know How to Articulate What We Need

In community, especially with people who love you, help will be offered up. This is, in fact, what God calls us to: "Bear one another's burdens, and so fulfill the law of Christ" (Gal. 6:2). If we are going to live out one of the primary principles of the gospel in loving one another, this presupposes that we are going to help the hurting. This is a fundamentally good thing; it's a God thing. The challenge is, in our grief we may not even know what we need. The secondary issue is that some of the people we are in community with think they have the answer. Did I mention community can be messy? We've already touched on this extensively, but we are not a people comfortable with pain, not for ourselves and not for those we care about.

Think about Job's friends with me for a moment. At first they show up and they do the right thing.

> Now when Job's three friends heard of all this evil that had come upon him, they came each from his own place, Eliphaz the Temanite, Bildad the Shuhite, and Zophar the Naamathite. They made an appointment together to come to show him sympathy and comfort him. And when they saw him from a distance, they did not recognize him. And they raised their voices and wept, and they tore their robes and sprinkled dust on their heads toward heaven. And they sat with him on the ground seven days and seven nights, and no one spoke a word to him, for they saw that his suffering was very great. (Job 2:11-13)

The problems arise when the friends open their mouths. Job had just suffered incredible loss. There's no way he can articulate what he needs, hence sitting in silence for seven days. The idea of connection and help can feel daunting when we ourselves aren't able to put together all of the pieces.

We See Ourselves as a Burden

"I just don't want to be a burden." Have you said these words? Are you saying these words? When something is unresolved in our lives and it continues to go unresolved, we can feel as though our very presence is burdensome. We can also feel like we don't fit in or don't have a place at the table. This is a lie intended to isolate us, and it's a strong one at that. I had a conversation with a friend last week who is walking through their own form of invisible grief. I could tell they were reluctant to even get on the phone with me, and when we did connect they were hesitant to share. I knew them well enough to finally just ask, "Why aren't you telling me what's going on?" The answer was simple and honest: "I just don't want to be a burden." I was quick to respond, "You are not a burden, you are a friend."

In the ongoing rhythm of our walk with Jesus, if God invites us to bear one another's burdens then we must also embrace the sacred act of letting others carry ours. To do otherwise is to miss out on a profound layer of community that Jesus envisioned—a dance of vulnerability and strength within the fabric of our shared faith. You are not a burden and there is a place for you at the table. Don't fall into the trap of comparison analysis; fall into the rest that comes in being with God's people.

We Are Overly Independent and Proud

In our modern world, we often idolize independence. We're taught that it's a virtue, this idea that we should be self-sufficient and not need the help of others. It goes without saying that this way of thinking can make its way into our grief. We sometimes carry this belief into our faith, thinking, "It's just me and God, and that's enough." While personal faith is crucial, this notion leaves out the communal aspect of what it means to follow Jesus. "Yes but, Drew, they don't understand. They don't get what I'm really going through." To some degree this may be true, and to expect others to fully relate is an unhealthy and often unrealistic practice. It's common to shy away from community when we're grieving, thinking no one gets it or we'll step into awkwardness and platitudes. But remember, the heart of community isn't flawless empathy; it's presence. Yes, people may not always know what to say or how to say it, but they can still love you well. They can still reflect the relational and nurturing nature of God even as both parties simply show up.

But let's be honest, opening up about something so painful can be hard. It's a reminder that we are weak and in need, and we can be quick to push back against this notion. It feels easier to keep our struggles to ourselves or between us and God. Yet the repetition of connection, confession, and prayer with each other, as James 5:16 suggests, isn't there by accident.

> Therefore confess your sins to each other and pray for each other so that you may be healed. The prayer of a righteous person is powerful and effective (James 5:16 NIV).

To confess our sins to one another brings incredible humility, and to pray for one another as we may struggle and have need calms our pride and is deeply effective. In our grief we are weak, and in need, but inside God's gift of community we are not left to fend for ourselves.

GOSPEL COMMUNITY IS A CONDUIT OF GRACE

It was one of those nights I mentioned above. Laura and I were set to host our community group and it had been a rough day. Neither one of us felt like we had much to offer but it was too late to change course. As people arrived and we shared a meal and then we made our way to the living room for discussion and prayer, I was simply going through the motions of facilitating and I knew it. All I wanted was to wrap things up so we could be alone. In every fiber of my being I wanted to isolate. Like a bear waiting for winter, I was ready to detach and hibernate, hoping spring held better fortune.

I can't tell you what the discussion topic was that night or what passage of Scripture we were unpacking, I can only tell you what one person shared. It's such a vivid memory that I could literally map out our living room that night. We would share requests and pray accordingly. Because I felt tired and the day was heavy, I approached this time completely unfiltered. I shared that we were struggling with our unmet desire for children and we could use prayer.

Sarah spoke up. She affirmed what we were feeling but then she spoke these words to us: "The LORD is near to the brokenhearted and saves the crushed in spirit." I knew these words from Psalm 34:18, I had read them dozens of times, but in that moment they hit differently. It was exactly what Laura and I needed to hear. It wasn't a fix and it didn't change what we were walking through, but it was a reminder we needed. God was with us and would, someway, somehow, redeem these years. In that moment, on that night (and many others), this community served as a conduit of grace to our tired hearts.

The entire concept of grace presupposes support: What we cannot do on our own, another does on our behalf without dropping a bill on our doorstep. I wonder if you're familiar with "talking trees." In an article from *National Geographic*, Daisy Chung and Ryan T. Williams explained and illustrated that there is a vast level of communication and support happening below the surface of forest soil. Taller, older trees are able to share their excess resources with other small, vulnerable trees to help support their continued growth. A struggling sapling is able to borrow what they are lacking in this interconnected web of underground community.[1]

This highlights the concept of borrowed faith. In certain seasons and under the constant weight of our invisible grief, our faith may wane. We, like the sapling, may need to borrow the faith of another. In Ecclesiastes 4, there's an echo of this beautiful truth: "Two are better than one, because they have a good reward for their toil" (v. 9). It resonates deeply with the essence of relational faith, especially when we face those seasons where our own belief falters. Sometimes, as we walk through valleys shadowed with doubt and disillusionment, there are moments when our faith feels like a flickering flame on the verge of being snuffed out. It's in these moments that borrowed faith becomes a lifeline.

The concept—when your faith is worn thin, you're carried by the faith of another. This isn't weakness; it's God's design. It's a beacon in the night shouting that life wasn't meant to be navigated alone! The biblical wisdom holds that "if either of them falls, one can help the other up." How countercultural to rely on someone else, yet how deeply biblical and grace-filled.

In this wonderful exchange, Ecclesiastes 4:12 becomes a powerful reminder: "And though a man might prevail against one who is alone, two will withstand him—a threefold cord is not quickly broken." When we interlace our lives with other burden bearers, we find strength beyond ourselves. This is gospel community's sacred alchemy—a mysterious, holy intertwining where we are able to stand firm in Jesus as we borrow the faith of another.

GOSPEL COMMUNITY IS NECCESARY FOR HEALING

There are different degrees of community as there are different degrees of friendship. I like to break these down by wave, handshake, and hug. Think of the wave as the larger community, maybe a church body. You are gathered and you are scattered, you are familiar but not as personally known. Then you have the handshake. This might be similar to a community group. You know each other on a more personal level and there is trust in these relationships. You feel comfortable opening up to a degree and they feel the same with you. Then you have the hug. With each degree the community grows smaller and this is by far the most intimate form. These are the gutter buddies, the 2 a.m. friends, the ones who know you best because you've shared the most. Even if you don't share DNA, this community is family in the truest sense. These are the people you go to for constant counsel and vice versa.

We need all of these expressions of gospel community as we walk through our grief and move toward healing. Each degree of community plays an important role and it's also important that we recognize the role they play in our life so that we can use wisdom as we steward our grief. Without a doubt, my friend, gospel community is necessary for healing. It not only helps lift the weight, but it also helps move us toward health, and serves as a re-interpreter in the midst of our pain and loss.

Tearing the Roof Off

In Mark 2 we get an amazing account of Jesus healing a paralytic man. His community of brothers would not allow anything to get in the way of getting this man to Jesus. They would serve as his arms. They would serve as his legs. They would literally carry him to Jesus. This is the power of gospel community on full display. Look at this passage:

> And when he returned to Capernaum after some days, it was reported that he was at home. And many were gathered together, so that there was no more room, not even at the door. And he was preaching the word to them. And they came, bringing to him a paralytic carried by four men. And when they could not get near him because of the crowd, they removed the roof above him, and when they had made an opening, they let down the bed on which the paralytic lay. And when Jesus saw their faith, he said to the paralytic, "Son, your sins are forgiven" (Mark 2:1-5).

In carrying this man to Jesus, they are essentially pushing him toward health. They desperately want to see healing in this man's life. Genuine, authentic gospel community will want the same for you. They will pray for you, plead for you, walk with you, and, at times, walk for you. These kinds of Jesus-loving friends will first and foremost pay attention to us as this is the first act of love, and then they will help move us forward with great care. Henri Nouwen frequently spoke about community and its healing power. In *Out of Solitude,* he writes, "When we honestly ask ourselves which person in our lives means the most to us, we often find that it is those who, instead of giving advice, solutions, or cures, have chosen rather to share our pain and touch our wounds with a warm and tender hand."[2] These four men were the paralytic's wounded healers. Their friend's hurting meant they hurt. We are not talking about those who try to push us toward health and healing by simply offering up unsolicited suggestions or telling us it's time to move on. These are not wounded healers, these are healers who wound. These men are not that. They are willing to literally tear the roof off a home to get this man to Jesus. Do you have this kind of community? Do you have brothers and sisters who truly know you, love you, and are willing to help move you toward healing, move you toward Jesus?

I love the response Jesus gives when He witnesses what I'm sure were moments of chaos as the roof came off and the man came down. As He takes in the faith of these four friends He says, "Son, your sins are forgiven." Notice He doesn't lead with, "Son, you are healed." Even more than physical healing, what this man truly needed was spiritual healing. It wasn't that Jesus didn't care about the physical challenges this man had; He did and He shows that by giving him the ability to walk. Jesus uses this opportunity to reframe our understanding and remind us that true healing doesn't come through a change of circumstance, it comes through a change of heart. The grace-filled, love-saturated, gospel community doesn't just bandage your wounds; it gently nudges you towards true healing, which, at its core, is a journey to Jesus Himself. As theologian John Stott writes, "The Christian community is a community of the cross, for it has been brought into being by the cross, and the focus of its worship is the Lamb once slain, now glorified."[3] Your healing isn't an aimless wandering—it's a guided path back to the heart of God. Every act of kindness, every embrace, every moment of shared sorrow and joy within this community is a divine echo, a reminder that Jesus is right there with you through it all. So, as you lean in to this grace-filled space, know that you're being drawn ever closer to the one who loved you first.

Meaning Makers and Reinterpreters

Imagine taking a trip to another country where you don't speak the language. Let's also pretend that translation apps don't exist. You can try to go it alone and take on all of the risks and challenges associated, or you can allow someone to interpret for you. As someone who has a legitimate fear of being locked up abroad, I'll choose door number two.

Paul David Tripp says that we are all "meaning makers." He says, "Every human being is a meaning maker, a theologian, a philosopher, or an anthropologist, always taking things apart to understand what they mean."[4] In our grief, we are interpreting a circumstance, an event, a reality. We are asking the questions, "What happened? Why did it happen?" and we are coming up with answers. The problem is we aren't always the best interpreters and in the fog of our own grief we can come to some incredibly flawed conclusions. We need others who love us and love Jesus to help us reinterpret our grief. We know our tendency to make grief our identity. Gospel community helps by stepping in and reinterprets, reminding us that we are in Christ, We know the temptation to believe lies about our grief. Gospel community helps reinterpret by gently recounting God's truth. We know the challenge of seeing purpose in our pain, wondering if it's all been a waste. Gospel community reinterprets the doubt by reminding us of God's promises to His kids. We need reinterpreters: the risk of being the sole meaning maker is far too great.

A few years ago I got hooked on the reality show, *Alone*. The premise of the show is pretty straight-forward. Experienced survivalists are dropped into a remote part of Canada with limited supplies and given the task to survive alone for as long as they can. The person who is able to withstand the elements and endure complete solitude the longest receives half a million dollars.

If you need even further confirmation that we weren't meant to be alone just watch a season of this show. For some who were fully confident they could stay in the wilderness at least a month, all it takes is one day for them to become mentally defeated and retreat. For others, you get to watch as excitement turns to desperation and determination to despair. As someone who loves the physiological aspects of an experiment like this, there are moments that are heartbreaking as people become so isolated and lonely that they begin to lose their grip on their emotions. All of a sudden seemingly small problems from the viewers' standpoint become disproportionately troublesome to the lone participant. You watch as fear begins to creep in, mental and emotional strength break down, and the impact of loneliness takes over. How different things would be if they weren't alone, if they had someone to come alongside and share the burden, to reinterpret.

Research consistently shows that social isolation and loneliness have significant negative impacts on both mental and physical health, including increased risks for depression, anxiety, heart disease, stroke, cognitive decline, a weakened immune system, and even premature death.[5] We were not built to go it alone. In the middle of life's storm, as the rain spits without reprieve, having a friend, having community, changes everything.

WE ARE BETTER TOGETHER

I love the movie *Grumpy Old Men* starring Walter Matthau and Jack Lemon. It's a classic. Here you find two old men, both widowers and both neighbors who drive each other crazy. Throughout the movie and throughout their relationship, they teeter back and forth between frustration and resentment to heartfelt care. There is constant tension, and yet when all is said and done they realize they are better together. They are indeed dear friends.[6] I see invisible grief and community in a similar light. Sometimes the two will seem combative, and at other times their friendship is a gift worth its weight in gold. Yes it's messy, but it's also beautiful and something all of us were made for, no matter the season or circumstance. You were never meant to do it alone. In the complex orchestration of God's design for humanity, we were made to be with one another. We need one another. I need you and you need me. I need you to pursue with presence and point me back to Jesus time and time again. You need me to lift your cot, tear the roof off, and lay you at Jesus' feet.

I say this with absolute conviction as one who knows. To sit in our grief and exist outside of community is to overlook one of God's most extraordinary gifts. It's within this perfectly imperfect melding of sufferers that we encounter the profound reminder that we are loved and the absolute assurance that we are never truly alone. In this space that must never become normative, where our stories intertwine, we are reminded that we are not swallowed by anonymity; rather, we are fully seen and genuinely loved.

REFLECTIONS

1. Are you in gospel community? If you are, what does that look like?

2. Even though gospel community can be messy, why is it still such an important piece of moving through our grief toward healing?

3. Who has come around you and what has it meant to you? Write down names and how that person has loved, encouraged, supported you.

4. Have you shared your grief and allowed others to be burden bearers? If not, what does it look like to take that step in the coming days and weeks?

IN JOY AND GRIEF

A HOSTAGE SITUATION

Pain and loss have been known to craft chains of fear and distrust, binding us tightly and seeking to keep us prisoners of our circumstances. Take, for instance, Heathcliff from Emily Brontë's *Wuthering Heights*. Heathcliff is a complex and enigmatic character whose life is marked by intense emotions and long-standing grievances. Found as a small orphan on the streets of Liverpool by Mr. Earnshaw, Heathcliff is brought to live at Wuthering Heights. Though initially favored by Mr. Earnshaw, he is later subjected to harsh treatment by the other Earnshaw child, Hindley.

Heathcliff's love for Catherine Earnshaw is the central focus of his life. Raised together, they form a deep, albeit tumultuous, bond, one that transcends a typical romantic attachment and becomes something all-consuming for Heathcliff. However, circumstances and social class differences come between them. Catherine chooses to marry Edgar Linton, a refined gentleman, believing that this union would elevate her status. Despite professing deep love for Heathcliff, she makes a pragmatic decision that devastates him.

This rejection leads Heathcliff to depart from Wuthering Heights, returning years later as a wealthy and determined man. However, instead of moving on, Heathcliff's undying love for Catherine turns into an obsession, laden with vengeance. He systematically ruins the lives of those around him whom he associates with his loss.

Catherine's untimely death further entraps Heathcliff in his grief and resentment. Rather than finding closure, her death intensifies his bitterness and longing, as she was the singular source of profound love and connection in his life. In his later years, Heathcliff becomes increasingly tormented, haunted by visions of Catherine, to the point where it consumes his entire existence.[1] This is Satan's desire, to consume our entire existence with pain. Satan aims to bind us in the shadows of our grief, whispering hopelessness so that we never step into the light where healing and hope await. Pain and loss become cruel captors, lacking any semblance of grace or willingness to negotiate a hostage release. The grief becomes an all-encompassing, driving force that wants to choose each step of our life moving forward or else hold us back completely.

How do we avoid this captor, and how do we move forward in a way that honors God but also does not dismiss our grief?

FROM WOUNDS TO SCARS

I have several visible scars on my body, each telling a story. On my left wrist you can see two small marks from where my hamster bit me when I was a child. On the outside of my right knee is proof that stretching out to catch a football on concrete might not have been the best idea. In between both eyebrows is a scar resembling a lightning bolt, a constant reminder that even at a church picnic a soccer ball to the face hits hard. Here's the thing about scars, they are a sign that healing has taken place. Some are barely visible, others have left a clear, twisted mark, but each has a story. Scars are stories that no longer have open wounds with only pain to share.

If we believe that there is purpose in our pain and the entirety of our life is wrapped in God's promise, then we must also see that this comes with an invitation to keep moving forward, to keep looking upward. Even in the reality of our pain and loss and the wounds they bring, we were never meant to set up camp and make grief our home. If Jeremiah 29:11 is true and God has a hope and future for His children, it is reasonable to conclude that this means we can walk forward into the future with hope. And the only way this is possible is when we begin to heal. This doesn't mean erasing the past, it doesn't mean ignoring the present; it means wounds becoming scars. How do we know we're healing and how do we get there? In all of my years walking alongside others in their grief, this has been one of the most prominent questions. In my own life this is a question I have asked many times.

Healing is a process. It doesn't happen overnight, especially when it comes to invisible grief. You might ask, is it even possible to heal when the pain and loss are just as real and just as present? Although it might seem like a distant journey, overwhelming and daunting, by the grace of God healing is not only possible for you (yes you), it's God's desire for you. He not only takes you as you are, with skinned knees, bruises, a foul mouth, and dirt on your face, but He loves you far too much to leave you where you are. We need only take His hand.

I knew I was entering the process of healing when I realized I didn't need to avoid my grief or run from it. As I shared previously, this took a good chunk of time and some serious back and forth with God. However, when I started to get there, I found that I was able to engage with the grief in a way that didn't send me down a dark hole of despair, but actually allowed for healthy dialogue with myself, others, and God. I was able to investigate and ask questions like, "What has happened and what is God saying? What is happening and what is God doing?"

I knew I was healing when I could accept what was and what wasn't. I've shared this with many as I've come to realize it myself: acceptance isn't denial. We've already touched on this passage once in this book, but I want us to take one more look from a different angle. This was life-changing when it came to my own healing journey. I remember reading through 2 Corinthians and coming to chapter 12 where Paul says, in reference to his thorn in the flesh, "Three times I pleaded with the Lord about this, that it should leave me. But he said to me, 'My grace is sufficient for you, for my power is made perfect in weakness.' Therefore I will boast all the more gladly of my weaknesses, so that the power of Christ may rest upon me" (2 Cor. 12:8-9). Paul wasn't denying the painful and problematic circumstance, he was instead accepting two things: the ongoing presence of the pain, and the sufficiency of God's grace. He came to the conclusion that the thorn was something he would have to live with, but in his weakness he would continue to move forward, knowing that the grace of God and power of Christ were moving in him, and were with him. Not only would Paul move forward, he says that he will now boast in his weakness! In doing so he is demonstrating a powerful part of the healing process—surrender. A wounded heart moves toward healing when it goes from "take this from me" to "I give this to you."

AN OFFERING

I recently connected with Annarina after I came across her story on Instagram. She's thirty-four and works with one of HTB's church plants in Malaysia, and recently she shared about her incredibly strong desire for marriage, a desire that continues to go unmet.

> Singleness was fun for a season, but then the thought of "what if this is true for all my life?" seemed really sad and made me ask, "how can this be an abundant life?" For me, that was really uncomfortable and made me nervous about missing out on a future with marriage and children. I prayed that if this was God's plan for me, instead of trying to hold Him ransom or twist His arm, He would just take this desire, this overwhelming desire for marriage and children away from me so that I can actually be happy in my singleness.

Annarina knew this wasn't really the prayer God wanted from her. As she shared, God didn't need her to give up her desire for marriage and simply be content.

> Contentment is great and it can help ground you, but what I realized is God has more than contentment for me. He's actually able to satisfy me even in my circumstances. He wasn't trying to get me to not desire marriage, instead He wanted me to take that desire and offer it at His feet as an offering and leave it to Him, so I wouldn't make an idol out of marriage which I would have done. I feel like God gave me a big beautiful vision of singleness by filling my life and spaces with things I would have never seen on my own. I know I am loved and known, and able to love others. I'm no longer afraid of the future and possibility of not being married. I know He's not going to short-change me. I know He has good for me, no matter what that looks like or doesn't look like.

I love this perspective from Annarina. It reminds me of the words of Spurgeon from a sermon he delivered on the book of Job, "My dear friend, when grief presses you to the dust, worship there."[2] I've been asked this a lot: "How do I know when I need to let the dream die?" My response is always the same: "Does it need to die or do you need to hand it over?" Unless, or until, God makes it clear that He has a definitively different plan, I don't believe we have to let our hopes, desires, or dreams die because, in fact, we are often talking about God-given desires. We don't need to take an axe to them and toss them into a fire to warm back our hearts, we just need to lay them at the feet of Jesus. Just as Abraham laid his precious son Isaac on the altar, in essence saying, "God, my son is ultimately your son," so too we need to lay all our desires, hopes, and dreams on the altar. In this act of worship, we release the need for control as we trust more fully in God's goodness. We release the need to hold on to something we have no control over and offer it up to the one who is the very definition of control. I've watched far too many people go the other route and start to pull away from God completely, entering a dark chapter of complete deconstruction when grief presses them into the dust.

Two summers during college I stayed with my oldest brother and sister-in-law outside of Atlanta. My brother Troy is the definition of an entrepreneur. Among other ventures was buying, renovating, and then selling or renting older homes in the area. I spent my weekends helping with these projects and loved every minute of it. Not only did I learn how to change electrical outlets without going full electric myself, I also grew an appreciation for the solid structure and foundation of many of these homes that were built upwards of 100 years ago. Like a testament to time, they are a steadfast presence that speaks of enduring strength and quiet resilience. Built with care and craftsmanship, they have weathered seasons and witnessed the world changing around them, firmly holding the house in a gentle, unyielding embrace. Each stone and beam tells a story, whispered in the language of hard work and patience, resonating with strength formed through trials. It could be tempting to walk through, look at the wear and tear, and come to the conclusion that the entire house needs to be taken to the studs and the foundation jackhammered and re-poured.

The longer we experience grief, the more we may be tempted to think that our faith, like an old house, needs to experience a complete overhaul, a demolition where only rubble remains. We live in a Christian era of deconstruction, where we pull apart our beliefs brick by brick when we don't get the response from God we're looking for or when we can't master the mind of God (as if we ever could) and account for all of His actions. We table faith and trust, recycle absolute truth, and become victims of circumstance. This grieves my heart as I've watched dear friends, dealt a poor hand, walk away from a faith that they once held so dear. In reality, yes, there may be a room or two in the house that needs attention, but overall the bones are good. If your faith has Jesus and God's grace at the center, let me assure you that the bones are good. Friend, you don't need to deconstruct your faith in order to deconstruct your grief. There will always be rooms to work on, paint to touch up, stairs that need mending. Our faith is always in process and in that process, in our heart, there is a room called grief where God is continually at work. There, He is mending wounds and forming scars, creating a place of worship where we bring our deepest desires as an offering and lay them down at the master's feet to do with as He will.

This shift that Annarina has come to in her own journey is one of the greatest signs of healing: the ability to walk forward with both joy and grief.

JOY AND GRIEF: TWO PEDALS, ONE BIKE

My grandparents bought me my first bicycle. It was bright red and they found it at a garage sale. I remember going to their house and being ecstatic as I looked at this glorious piece of machinery with its paint chipping and tires worn. I faintly remember being offered help in learning to ride it but quickly resisting as I pulled one leg over the middle bar, foot planted on the pedal, beaming with wild and reckless confidence. In a matter of minutes I turned the bike over into a pile of rocks and, with head laid low, made my way inside to clean gravel from my new wounds. It turns out balance is an important part of riding a bike successfully, something I'm admittedly still not great at. Many years later I would have the grand idea to buy a road bike to get back and forth from work in Atlanta. It did not go well. You know how some people veer away from vehicles and hug the shoulder of the road? I was the opposite. I quickly sold the bike in an attempt to save face, both literally and figuratively.

For me, the hardest part of learning to ride that bicycle back in the summer of 1990 was figuring out how to operate both pedals. Once I did that, I was able to slowly but surely move forward.

When I think about living with invisible grief, I think about the two pedals on that bike. On one side we have grief, an uninvited guest, yet very real. On the other side is joy, something we desperately want but aren't sure is truly possible. Many of us have become convinced that it has to be one or the other, that these cannot coexist. Guilt and fear are often at the core of this belief. We tell ourselves that to experience joy in the midst of grief would be ignoring the pain and minimizing the loss. On the other hand, to continue to experience grief and give it recognition means a lack of gratitude to God for the good in my life. We treat joy and grief like mutually exclusive relationships and walk with fear of one meeting the other. We buy into the lie that joy must put grief to death or that grief will inevitably mean living a joyless existence. Laura and I cycled between these for years and all it really led to was tired delusion and confusion. Why? Because we are not meant to live segmented lives where we pack away pieces of ourselves in a sad attempt to present the best version of ourselves. This is the antithesis of the gospel, which calls us to come as we are in all of our messiness and malaise.

A healing heart starts to understand that moving forward in hope means moving forward holding both joy in one hand and grief in the other. This is the most authentic, honest way. This is what it means to be a good steward of our grief. We are able to stop seeing it as an obstacle for joy and care for it. Instead of running from or burying our grief, we are able to acknowledge that God can, and will, use it for good in our lives and in the lives of others. It's not something to waste. Instead of seeing our grief as a scarlet letter, we respect it for what it is and look to live in a way that recognizes and honors both our pain and God's ability to heal in a way that produces lasting joy, a non-circumstantial state of being where lasting hope and peace reside.

JOY AND GRIEF: THE PRACTICE OF LAMENT

In the first pages of this book, we touched on the concept of lamenting and how foreign this practice has become in our western world. I can't emphasize enough how important the ability to lament is to the process of our healing, of our wounds becoming scars. With all of the spiritual disciplines in which we can take part to grow in our faith, I believe without reservation that lamenting is the spiritual discipline of grief. Sure, we're happy to talk about and put into practice the other disciplines: prayer, solitude, Bible reading, worship, service, confession, fellowship. When it comes to regularly practicing, becoming familiar with, and dare I say becoming *good* at lamenting, there are few takers. This is the last kid picked for dodgeball on the playground. It's the ugly crier that you don't make eye contact with. It's the…okay, you get the point. Let me just say it this way without pretense: in order to truly heal we need to make friends with lamenting.

Whether this looks like a daily or weekly practice, make sure it's a regular practice for as long as you have invisible grief in your life. If this is a long season, allow lamenting to be a part of that season. If your grief is for a lifetime, allow lamenting to find a permanent place as you walk forward.

TURN, ASK, TRUST

I want to propose a very simple but effective process of putting this into practice. If you remember from the chapter "Okay to Not Be Okay," we looked at Psalm 13 and David's ability to be brutally honest with God. Watch that play out again here as we walk out these three steps of lamenting.

Turn

Some of us only turn outward or inward when we are suffering. We take what we're experiencing, what we're feeling, and what we're wrestling with to someone else, or we go inward and talk to ourselves. These aren't bad conversations but they can't be the only conversation or even the most important. Lamenting means turning to God and bringing the complaint to Him, articulating the pain. We take the crux of the problem that has caused our pain and loss and bring it to Him.

> How long, O LORD? Will you forget me forever?
> How long will you hide your face from me?
> How long must I take counsel in my soul
>   and have sorrow in my heart all the day?
> How long shall my enemy be exalted over me? (Ps. 13: 1-2)

Ask

What is the bold ask? God welcomes this from His children without the need to caveat. If it's the spouse, ask. If it's children, ask. If it's peace with past trauma, ask. If it's mental or physical healing, ask. If it's a God-given desire, a good hope, a good dream, ask. As James says, "You do not have because you do not ask God" (James 4:2b NIV). If your motives are good, then ask.

> Consider and answer me, O LORD my God;
>   light up my eyes, lest I sleep the sleep of death,
> lest my enemy say, "I have prevailed over him,"
>   lest my foes rejoice because I am shaken (Ps. 13: 3-4).

Trust

As we talked about in the last chapter, even though we, like Paul says in 1 Corinthians 13:12, "see in a mirror dimly" when it comes to our full knowledge and understanding of God, His ways, His plans, His purpose, we affirm in our being that He is worthy of our trust and our worship, as we remember His goodness.

> But I have trusted in your steadfast love;
>   my heart shall rejoice in your salvation.
> I will sing to the LORD,
>   because he has dealt bountifully with me. (Ps. 13:5-6)

Barry Webb describes the book of Lamentations as "ordered messiness." I would say the same for our practice of lamenting as a spiritual discipline in our grief. It is an ordered messiness that deeply connects us with an orderly God who gladly enters into the mess with ointment, balm, and gauze as we look to heal.

JOY AND GRIEF: LOVE AGAIN TAKES ROOT

> Love is patient and kind; love does not envy or boast; it is not arrogant or rude. It does not insist on its own way; it is not irritable or resentful; it does not rejoice at wrongdoing, but rejoices with the truth. Love bears all things, believes all things, hopes all things, endures all things. Love never ends (1 Cor. 13:4-8a).

Patient and Kind

Last week I was sitting on the back porch with Laura and she brought up how the reality of turning forty next year unearthed some grief. When grief was an open wound this could have sent her spiraling, but because it's now a scar, she was able to acknowledge it without becoming defeated or owned by it. There is a patience that comes with healing and there is a kindness. When you look at the word "grieve" in the original Greek, it's present tense. This is a great reminder that our grief isn't isolated to a single moment. Even as we journey through healing, the hidden undercurrents of our grief will inevitably resurface. They arrive like waves, each with its own unique intensity and timing. When these waves wash over you, acknowledge the pain and recognize the loss, but affirm that they do not wield power over you. In the words of John Piper, "Occasionally weep deeply over the life you hoped would be. Grieve the losses. Then wash your face. Trust God. And embrace the life you have."[3] Hone in on the word "occasionally" because unscheduled grief pop-ins will happen, an untimely knock on the door of your heart. When it does, no matter the reason, don't beat yourself up. You're not back at the starting line, you didn't go to jail without passing Go, this simply means you're human, a human in need of ongoing grace. Frederick Beuchner speaks to this in his book *Crazy, Holy Grace.*

> Every person we have ever known, every place we have ever seen, everything that has ever happened to us—it all lives and breathes deep in us somewhere whether we like it or not, and sometimes it doesn't take much to bring it back to the surface in bits and pieces. A scrap of some song that was popular years ago. A book we read as a child. A stretch of road we used to travel. An old photograph, an old letter. There is no telling what trivial thing may do it, and then suddenly, there it all is.[4]

It Does Not Envy

A healing heart pushes back against bitterness and overly protective pessimism, opening the door to curiosity and possibility. When my infertility was an open wound I found it incredibly difficult to be around pregnant people. I wanted what they had and at times the roots of bitterness, longing for sun and water, found nourishment in my grief. Because I wasn't at a place to make peace with the pain, I had trouble making peace with others who stood in the place I desperately longed to be. For this to change, I had to come to a place of recognition.

There are some experiences in life we simply have to make peace with in order to heal. Our grief is one of those. If your life is a rope, there are certain knots we don't get to untangle this side of heaven. This is obviously difficult, as we live in a world that wants to have good and rational justification for every single thing that happens, but not all of life works that way. To make peace with the pain—not hiding it away, not ignoring it, not denying it—is an act of faith.

It Rejoices With the Truth

Gratitude is an important part of healing, but gratitude must be rightly defined. Every morning when I wake up I lay in bed and I thank God for things in my life. I thank Him for Laura, I thank Him for another day of waking up, I thank Him for our home, I thank Him for my son, I thank Him for drinks in the fridge and food in the pantry. I thank Him for putting up with someone like me. I do this regardless of how I feel. There are many mornings I don't feel grateful. Herein lies the rub. Gratitude is not a feeling but a recognition of what is; It's the opportunity to worship God for who He is and what He has provided. In our grief, when we hear people say, "You just need to be grateful" what we interpret is, "You just need to stop being sad." This is a false understanding. Regardless of our feelings, when we are able to open our eyes to the good provision around us it's a beautiful reminder that our grief is not the whole of the story. Set feelings aside for a moment. Look around. What can you be grateful for? Think small, think basic and thank God. If grief is going to come knocking at the door day after day and we want joy to answer it, we need to let gratitude help with the lock.

Love Bears All Things

Notice the verse doesn't say *we* bear all things; it says *love* bears all things. This is a love that isn't birthed from within us, it's a love that is placed in us through the grace of Jesus. This is the blood of our savior coursing through our veins and making it possible and plausible for us to keep standing in life's most torrential downpour. When the apostle Paul pleads for relief but instead finds reasons to boast, uttering the words, "grace is sufficient" it's because the love of Christ has become a powerful antibiotic and healing agent to His wounds (2 Cor. 12:9). It's this sufficient grace that leads us to praise instead of panic, trust instead of torment, love instead of indifference, and hope that transcends even the greatest heartache.

In the ragged and raw moments of our daily lives, there is a truth that whispers through the chaos if we're quiet enough to hear it—God's grace is not just a nice idea, but our daily bread. We stumble through days that batter and bruise us, trying so desperately to hold it all together, while beneath the surface there's a sacred truth trembling with hope: His grace is sufficient, and this is extravagant.

Every single day, it's the grace that wraps around us when we're most shattered, the tender mercy that finds us in the messes of our making and loves us still. This grace looks past our sad attempt at self-sufficiency and leans into our weaknesses, meeting us right there with God saying, "Yes, even here."

We're all beggars at the gate, hands extended, needing what we cannot provide for ourselves. In that need, we find His sufficiency inexplicably holding us together, smoothing the jagged edges, flooding the darkness with light. So, allow yourself to be embraced in this relentless grace. It's a perpetual reminder that we're already fully loved and free— no masks or pretenses necessary. This is where healing is, where hope abounds, and where love eternally reigns.

Love Hopes All Things

This is the last phrase I want to draw our attention to. I was talking with my good friend and fellow pastor Ryan about this not too long ago. We were discussing the need to "watch for the vows" as an indicator that a wound is still very much open. This is cause and effect language. Because of this, I'll never that. Because of this, I'll always that. In an effort to protect, we put up safeguards around our heart. The problem is in doing so we also lock hope out of our foreseeable future. To heal is to hope.

PUTTING IT ALL TOGETHER

If walking with joy and grief is the way forward for the healing heart, how do we get there? Let me pause for one minute and express this with as much simplicity as possible: human-made initiatives will only lead to human-made results. We will not heal by white-knuckling; we will not heal through a set of rigid rules or emotional regulations. Without holy reliance and holy surrender we are attempting the equivalent of climbing Mount Everest in flip flops. Healing, true healing, must come through the power of the Holy Spirit within us. Healing of the heart, soul, and mind is a divine work, not a human-made equation. With that in mind, we put down and we pick up as we move forward. We retrace our steps, going as far back as necessary, as we trust God will meet us there.

- We put down the temptation to run.
- We put down the lies we are tempted to believe, especially the insidious whispers that tell us God is indifferent to our suffering.
- We pick up the invitation to come with honest emotions, honest questions, honest pleas before a God who says "child, come as you are."
- We pick up our true identity, found not in our grief but in Christ, as sons and daughters of a loving Father who sees with compassion and knows us completely.

- We allow God to pick us up and remind us that even in the pain, even in the aching chapters of our lives, we are cradled by God with purpose and promise, wrapped in the power of the gospel.

- We don't go it alone. Instead, we learn to lean on our brothers and sisters to help bear the burden, advocate on our behalf, sit in the dark, and gently point us to the one who is close to the brokenhearted and saves those crushed in Spirit (Ps. 34:18). His name none other than Jesus.

And in all of this, as we take each step forward, we do so with Heaven in our sights.

JOY AND GRIEF: A PROPER PERSPECTIVE

MEET JOANNA

I first met Joanna around 2015 when she started attending the church I was pastoring in Seattle. The thing I immediately appreciated about Joanna was that she didn't hide what she was thinking or how she was feeling. Doing ministry in a city that's known for being passive, this was refreshing. As I got to know Joanna she became more comfortable sharing her story. I remember sitting in a local coffee shop as she opened up about some of the things that were unique to her background and how they bled into her current reality.

At twenty-seven years old Joanna started having balance issues and headaches. She noticed an odd lump toward the back of her head. She went to the doctor and after the examination they were pretty sure it was just a fat or calcium deposit. They encouraged Joanna that it shouldn't be a problem, but if things didn't get better in a few weeks, to book a follow-up appointment. Things didn't get better. With the encouragement of her mother, she returned to the doctor. They decided to do a CAT scan. Joanna recalls it was the night of Halloween that she received the call. What the scan showed wasn't a fat or calcium deposit, it was a tumor in the lining of the brain. Two weeks later Joanna would find herself being prepped for surgery. Oh how things can change so quickly. They would go in to remove this fairly large tumor that was, in fact, pushing both in on the brain and out through the skull. The surgery was successful, but the side effects were great.

Over the next two decades, and to this very day, Joanna would suffer from memory issues, sensory issues, social challenges, and emotional imbalances. I would watch as some of this played out right before my eyes. Joanna keeps earbuds in and music on for most of the day when she's outside of her home. As she would put it, "The world is just too loud for me." Everyday is a struggle to find the balance between sensory exposure and sensory overload. On any given Sunday I would see Joanna have to leave our worship service as music played. While others lifted their voices and hands, Joanna would make her way to a bathroom stall and cry. Something she desperately wanted to take part in – the connected melody of family worship – was so meaningful and yet, for Joanna, so distant.

Beyond sensory issues, Joanna struggles with "cold storage" memory as she calls it. It's not that information isn't there in the brain, it's that it's hard to reach. Like a box at the very back of a storage closet, it takes time for Joanna to process. As if that weren't enough to try and manage, post-tumor Joanna doesn't remember most of her life. Her brain isn't able to keep a lot of memories, as the storage is limited. Along with memory digression and chronic headaches, waves of anxiety and depression have made themselves at home. All of these things combine to make connection and social interactions challenging at best.

Joanna is on disability, unable to work because of the effects that came with the brain tumor. Disability support only goes so far, especially in a city like Seattle where it costs one hundred bucks for a gallon of milk (okay, that might be a stretch). Limited funds, combined with mental and physical fatigue means Joanna ends up being by herself a lot. This isn't something she desires, it's something she grieves. Navigating relationships and functioning inside of community isn't a walk in the park, it's a trek through the jungle.

> At twenty-seven, when others are getting married, having children, starting exciting careers, it felt like someone put my life on pause but forgot to come back and push play. I struggled and still struggle with questions like "Am I only alive to feel pain? Have I accomplished anything in life? Is there a reason I'm still here?"

Like I said, I appreciate Joanna's honesty.

Joanna just turned fifty. We sat down and talked about her journey through invisible grief. She shows no outward physical manifestation of the pain and loss, only the inward war of mental untangling, emotional balancing, and sensory overload. All these serve as reminders of what has never been, and things that may never be. Here's what stood out to me most about our conversation. It wasn't the recounting of pain and suffering or the effects of the brain tumor. What stood out most was an immovable trust that's produced an incredible perspective.

> I'm never going to thank God for my brain tumor, but I will thank Him that He's able to take something as horrible as a brain tumor and still bring something good out of it. Throughout all of this, my faith has only

deepened because I know what's ahead. I really look forward to the new heavens and new earth more than I ever have before. People and creation will be back to how it was always meant to be. My head will be healed, people like Joni Earekson Tada will be able to do cartwheels. I have hope in Jesus now as I look ahead to that eternal future. It will all be as God intended all along.

In Joanna's life there is anticipation that has begun to take the pen and write her story. It's not a story of grief that ends with unrealized desires, loneliness, and despair. It's a story with a future—and a great one at that. The story being written is greater than any of the pain and loss that has come or will come. While the wait and the weight of grief aren't easy, there is something truly spectacular on the horizon for Joanna, for you and me, and for all the beloved children of God! It's time to look up!

HEAVEN IS IN OUR SIGHTS

> So we fix our eyes not on what is seen, but on what is unseen, since what is seen is temporary, but what is unseen is eternal (2 Cor. 4:18 NIV).

When it comes to legitimate healing, when it comes to being made truly whole, when it comes to walking with joy and grief, it's all about the destination in front of us and the one who is leading us there. Perspective is everything. If our eyes are only fixed on the here and now, even in the best this life has to offer we will be thoroughly disappointed and left wanting. I assure you I'm not saying any of this to appease you, to make light of everything we've talked about up to this point, or to put a shiny bow on what you're walking through. No, my dear brothers and sisters, I'm saying this because it is our greatest reality on the other side of salvation. We haven't just been saved *from* something, we've been saved *to* something. For the single, the barren, the abandoned, the physically, emotionally, and mentally broken, the wounded, and the wandering: we are headed home!

> There is great rejoicing in trials of many kinds
> When I am given over to resurrection life
> The glory that is coming is truly coming soon
> Jesus what an honour to suffer well with you[5]

This is how Paul, in all of his suffering, in all his heartache, could pen these words. "For I consider that the sufferings of this present time are not worth comparing with the glory that is to be revealed to us" (Rom. 8:18). Paul isn't minimizing the pain, he's maximizing the glory! As we walk day by day, we can lift our heads knowing that even our greatest pain falls miserably short of the wonderful expanse of God's infinite grace that lies ahead. Because our hope is in the resurrected Christ who will resurrect us in glory, even in death there is eternally tethered hope. "All death can do to Christians is make their lives infinitely better."[6] In Christ you are healed. In Christ—come hell or high water, even if your current circumstances never change—you are whole. This isn't a temporary wrap of gauze around the wound to keep us moving forward, it's the ultimate and final prognosis declaring that not only does our grief have a timestamp, absolute healing is ahead. And isn't the very essence of healing to take something broken and make it whole?

As I've written this section I've had one song on repeat. As we start to close out our conversation I want to share some of the lines with you. It's written by my good friends Zach Bolen and Brian Eichelberger.

> Heaven is in our sights
> Beauty beyond the skies

Heaven is in our sights, look up
Heaven is in our eyes
Sure as the morning light
Heaven is in our eyes, look up

We will outshine the sunrise
We will outlast the moon
Glorified in Your love light
Forever is all for You[7]

I don't know what God is going to do in your life, but I do know what He is going to do after this life for those who are in Christ. There is a book I read with Silas every night. I believe it to be one of the best books ever written: it's *The Jesus Storybook Bible* written by Sally Lloyd-Jones. It's a book written for children, a book that every adult should read. I want you to hear these words from the final pages, "A Dream of Heaven." More than that, I want you to read slowly and allow this reflection from Revelation 21 to wash over you, to clean your wounds, to gently lift your chin.

> And the King says, "Look!
> God and His children are together again.
> No more running or hiding.
> No more crying or being lonely or afraid.
> No more being sick or dying.
> Because all of those things are gone.
> Yes, they're gone forever.
> Everything sad has come untrue.
> And see—I have wiped away every tear from every eye!"[8]

It doesn't matter how many times I read these words, they never grow old and they only sink deeper into the depths of my soul. They bring me to tears as I envision the family reunion that's coming for you and for me. Children reunited with Abba, our Father, embraced by Jesus our Brother and savior. What a day that will be. As I close my eyes, I can see it. I can see Shelbi running and laughing. I can see Aaron being hugged by his heavenly Father. I can see Scott and Janet sitting and talking with Madison, no implant needed. I can see Nick for the first time embracing his wife and children, holding them close. I can see Sarah sitting in a field with all of the friends she poured into over the years. I can see Joanna taking in all of the sights and sounds, a smile beaming cheek to cheek. And I see Laura to my right and Silas to my left. We're walking hand in hand, fully whole, fully healed. And at the center of it all, Jesus. With a kind smile and outstretched arms saying, "Welcome home." God's promise fulfilled, every broken piece put back together, everything sad having come untrue. Take heart, my friend, even as we walk with and steward our grief in the here and now, this is where we are headed. This isn't a pipe dream; this is a promise for all of those who are in Christ, all of the broken and bruised, all of the misfits. We will be reunited with the one who has never left our side.

A FEW FINAL WORDS

I said it at the beginning, and I'll say it again now: it's an honor to share in this conversation with you. Thank you for taking the time and trusting me, to an extent, with your grief. I also want to thank everyone who shared their stories with me to share with you. Thank you for being vulnerable and open to share. I would also be remiss if I didn't thank my much better half, Laura. In every season, she has been a constant source of care, understanding, and encouragement, all wrapped in godly wisdom.

I pray that you know how much God loves you, just as you are. He doesn't need you to clean yourself up, Jesus has already taken care of that. I pray that His voice is the loudest in your life no matter what comes. I pray that His sufficient grace takes wounds to scars. I pray that every lie falls flat to the truth that in Christ you are seen, you are known, and you are loved, no matter what comes or what doesn't.

I want to end our time together by praying for you with these words from Hebrews 13:20-21. These are the same words, the same benediction, I offer to those I have the privilege of pastoring. With that, grace and peace to you, my newfound friend.

> Now may the God of peace who brought again from the dead our Lord Jesus, the great shepherd of the sheep, by the blood of the eternal covenant, equip you with everything good that you may do his will, working in us that which is pleasing in his sight, through Jesus Christ, to whom be glory forever and ever. Amen.

REFLECTIONS

1. On the spectrum of open wound to fully healed scar, where are you when it comes to your grief?

2. What did you think about Annarina's story of laying her desires down as an offering? Why is this an important part of healing? Are you there?

3. Why is having a heavenly perspective necessary when it comes to healing? Why is this so much more than putting a bandage on our grief?

4. What do you think about the concept of moving forward in both joy and grief, not one or the other? How is this freeing and how is it challenging?

HELPING THE HURTING

I wanted to take time to talk with my "wounded healers." Your role in the life of those walking with invisible grief is critically important and can't be understated. You are the community we talked about needing in order to begin healing, and really throughout every step of the healing process, as wounds become scars. Not only that, we need you after as well! This is not the easiest of endeavors. This isn't easy because it's unnatural. This isn't how God intended it when He first created and said it was good. Regardless, here we are and here you are. And thanks be to God you showed up.

In talking with people over the past year of writing this book, and over the past two decades of pastoral ministry, there are common themes that have made their way to the surface when it comes to helping the hurting. Before I share a list of do's and don'ts based on my own experience and that of my wife Laura and others, I just want to take a minute to thank you and encourage you. Thank you for caring. Seriously, thank you for caring for someone else enough to take the time to want to learn and grow so you can best support them. That alone means the world to me and people walking through their own grief.

THE DON'TS

Let's start with what not to do. I want to highlight three areas to steer clear of when it comes to helping those who are walking with invisible grief.

Don't Be Quick to Fix It

During our first year of marriage Laura and I lived in Atlanta. For whatever reason, my body didn't approve. It was a whole new set of allergens for me and that carried some incredibly delightful consequences. On several occasions during that first summer, a finger or toe would swell up without warning and for no apparent reason. This wasn't usually a big deal until one night I woke up with a very odd sensation coming from one of the fingers on my left hand. It just so happened that my ring finger was swollen, and yes, I was wearing my ring. In frustration, and not being so keen on the idea of losing a finger, I drove myself to the local ER. Apparently ring cutters are in high demand. The young attendant informed me that one of their cutters was broken and the other was being used at another location but would be there within the next one or two hours. I assumed we would wait for the proper device to arrive until I was called back to a room and approached with a small saw. In an attempt to get me out of the ER as quickly as possible and make more room for others, the young doctor attempted to saw off the ring. Eventually it worked but not without first cutting into my finger and requiring that I receive a tetanus shot. Good times.

We want to extinguish the pain as quickly as possible by whatever means possible. What we often don't take into account is the additional pain we may be causing by taking this approach. In an attempt to make burdens light we can unintentionally make light of the burden. This is a natural response given the quick-fix, keep-moving-forward, razor-thin-margin-of-time society we live in. We have to push back against this temptation.

Don't Project

The desire is good. We want to show that we can relate with the person in their grief. The problem is their grief is unique to them and unless we actually have walked through exactly what they are walking through, acting as if we totally understand what they're feeling or facing isn't actually helpful, it's dismissive and hurtful. As I began to heal, I started to give people the benefit of the doubt when this would happen. I knew they meant well. But for someone who has deep wounds, saying that you understand the pain and loss of their infertility because once you had dreams of becoming a doctor and it didn't pan out, is not the same and definitely does not help. Stay away from saying things like, "I totally get it." You probably don't and that's okay. I don't need you to, I just need you to be here with me.

Don't Make Their Pain the Center of Every Interaction

A few years ago I walked with a friend through a really difficult season. We would meet up every few weeks and take walks. A few months in he stopped me and said, "You know we don't have to talk about this every time we get together." Without realizing it I had made his pain and loss the central topic of every interaction we had. Sometimes those who are hurting just need to hang out. They just need to take in a movie. They need to laugh, have fun, be reminded that the grief doesn't define them. This also helps to prevent the idea that they're a project you've taken on, instead of a friend you truly care for.

THE DO'S

Alright, now let's move on to the good stuff. Here are three things people have done for me and for others that I believe are truly helpful and a reflection of Jesus Himself.

A Ministry of Presence—Be There

Jesus slowed down for people. He was fully present and without hurry. He was incredibly inefficient by the world's standards. He sat with the woman at the well, He sat and ate with sinners, He took time to attend to the outcast. Love demands we slow down. In his book *Three Mile an Hour God*, Kosuke Koyama expressed this very notion. "Love has its speed. It is a spiritual speed. It is a different kind of speed from the technological speed to which we are accustomed." If we are to be the hands and feet of Jesus to the hurting, we need to show up and keep showing up. As we do this, our posture must be unhurried so as to not give the impression that the individual is not really worth our undivided time and attention. This requires sacrifice, but that's what love is. It's inconvenient, won't always fit into our schedule, and will require long-suffering and patience.

Presence is a physical manifestation, yes, but that's only part of it. Most of us feel anxiety when we encounter a situation where we're not in control. When we sit with someone facing circumstantial grief, we want their pain and hurt to stop but quickly realize we don't have the power to make that happen. In order to be fully present, we must get comfortable with not being in control. Not only does this help us to be fully present, it also calms the person who is hurting as you give up the responsibility of making them better.

I want to make one sidenote here. Obviously you will not always be able to "be in the room." You have other priorities and responsibilities and don't need to feel guilt of that or set these aside. Being there in a literal sense is important and irreplaceable, but the act of regular check-ins over the phone, via text, etc. have their place as well. Even when you can't be there, be there.

Many times, the simple act of just being present, listening, and acknowledging a person's pain can be a healing balm to a hurting heart. Never underestimate the power of simply showing up.

Spirit-led Intuition

What often keeps us from being present or even the thinking of shouldering another person's pain is the fear of not knowing what to say. This is a common challenge. I can't tell you how many times I've felt the same way. The thought of stepping into someone's deepest pain and our mind goes blank, our words fall flat. This can be paralyzing. Let me encourage you. You don't need to have all of the answers, and you don't need to have the perfect words. You have God who goes with you. This is where we need to press into the presence of the Holy Spirit. During any pastoral counseling, any check-ins, follow-ups, or coffees with people who are walking through something painful, this is my prayer before and during: "Lord is there anything you want me to say, any encouragement to give, any question to ask?" Then I listen and trust that He's actually there among us and for us.

Speak Truth, Not Platitudes, and Not Too Soon

Here's what I can tell you for sure: when it comes to a person's pain and loss, speaking too soon can be (and often is) much more harmful than helpful, even if what you're saying is true. This is where I hit a roadblock early on in pastoral ministry. I couldn't connect the dots between truth and timing. I thought that as long as I was saying something true, the timing didn't really matter. I was wrong. When you're sitting with a person who just received a life-altering diagnosis, timing matters. When you're in the living room of a couple who just found out they can't have children, timing matters. When a young man comes to you completely broken because of the residual pain of being abandoned as a child, timing matters. A quick word will not only fall on deaf ears, it will pour salt in the wound as you unintentionally minimize the person's pain.

Not that we haven't hit this enough, but here's one more time for good measure. Please don't offer up things that simply aren't true, but sound good. Although well-intentioned, this is often a way for people who are uncomfortable with pain to offer a band-aid and move on. What hurting people don't need to hear is:

- "God is closing a door but opening a window."
- "What doesn't kill you makes you stronger."
- "God never gives us more than we can handle."
- "This was all a part of His plan."
- "Everything happens for a reason."

Now, is there a time and need to speak truth, especially encouraging truth? Absolutely. We need to hear that God has a good plan, that He hasn't turned His back on us. We need the loving words that we are not our grief, we are sons and daughters of God in Christ. We need to be reminded that through Jesus our future is purchased and that we're moving toward a day with no more pain and no more tears. But before those words come spilling out of our mouths, well-intentioned and all, take a minute to consider the possibility that what the person next to you might need in the moment, where the pain is still wet like a new coat of paint, isn't a word of encouragement (yet) but a present friend willing to sit with them and acknowledge their pain. Speak truth and encouragement, yes. But don't speak too soon. Allow the Holy Spirit to be your guide.

WE NEED YOU

Before we end this conversation, I'm reminded of these words from Proverbs 18:24, "A man of many companions may come to ruin, but there is a friend who sticks closer than a brother."

For those who are experiencing invisible grief, chances are there is a long season, maybe a lifetime ahead of walking this out. Many may come and go, but few will stick closer than a brother. We need you. We need you, parents; we need you, brothers and sisters; we need you grandparents; we need you, pastors; we need you, friends. You are a gift from God and a tangible reminder of His love, kindness, and grace. May God bless you as you bless others in their time of need.

NOTES

INTRODUCTION

1.   Frances, Allen, "When Good Grief Goes Bad," The Huffman Post, 2012, https://www.huffpost.com/entry/grief-depression_b_1301050.

CHAPTER 1

1.   *Prefontaine*, directed by Steve James, Hollywood Pictures, 1997.

2.   Bolen, Zach, "Illusion," *Fear,* Humble Beast, 2019.

3.   Keller, Tim, *Walking with God Through Pain and Suffering* (Dutton Publishing, 2013), p.26.

4.   Millacci, Tiffany Sauber, "7 Trauma Responses Types and How to Recognize Them." PositivePsychology.com, 2023, https://positivepsychology.com/trauma-response/.

5.   Kahan, Noah, "Growing Sideways," *Stick Season*, Mercury Records, 2022.

6.   Jimmy Eat World, "Pain," Futures, Interscope Records, 2004.

7.   Lewis, C. S., *The Problem of Pain*. (New York: HarperOne, 2001), p. 90.

8.   Manning, Brennan, *The Ragamuffin Gospel: Good News for the Bedraggled, Beat-Up, and Burnt Out* (Colorado Springs:Multnomah Publishers, 2000), p. 25.

9. See Siegel, Daniel, *The Power of Showing Up*. (Melbourne: Scribe Publications, 2020).

10. Lucado, Max, *Just Like Jesus: A Heart Like His*, (Nashville: Thomas Nelson, 2012), p. 3.

CHAPTER 2

1. Schwartz, Brad, "The Infamous, 'War of the Worlds,' Radio Broadcast Was a Magnificent Fluke." Smithsonian Magazine, 2015, https://www.smithsonianmag.com/history/infamous-war-worlds-radio-broadcast-was-magnificent-fluke-180955180/.

2. Harlow, Olivia, "Fun Facts About the Brain That will Blow Your Mind," Analog, 2024, https://legacybox.com/blogs/analog/25-brain-facts-blow-mind.

3. Fiedler, Klaus, Uli Hemmeter, and Carolin Hofmann, "The Origin of Illusory Correlations," *European Journal of Social Psychology, vol. 14, issue 2*, 1984.

4. Bowler, Kate, *Blessed: A History of the American Prosperity Gospel* (New York: Oxford Academic, 2013).

5. Peterson, Eugene H, *The Message: The Bible in Contemporary Language* (Colorado Springs: NavPress, 2002).

6. Solomon, Ashley, "Time Heals all Wounds and Other Falsehoods," Galia Collaborative, 2024, https://galiacollaborative.com/time-heals-all-wounds/.

7. Leftwich, Benjamin Francis, "Moon Landing Hoax," *Some Things Break*, Dirty Hit Records, 2024.

8. Kennedy, Rose, *Rose Fitzgerald Kennedy*, GoodReads, accessed April 2024, https://www.goodreads.com/quotes/140515-it-has-been-said-time-heals-all-wounds.

9. See "Fallacy of Relative Privation," Academy 4SC, accessed April 2024, https://academy4sc.org/video/fallacy-of-relative-privation-all-problems-are-relative/.

CHAPTER 3

1. See Nick Vujicic Biography. Nickvministries.org, accessed May 2024, https://nickvministries.org/about/nick-biography/.

2. Hanson, Rick, "Feeling Cared About," Rick Hanson, 2024, https://rickhanson.com/feel-cared-about/.

3. Manning, Brennan, *The Ragamuffin Gospel: Good News for the Bedraggled, Beat-Up, and Burnt Out* (Colorado Springs: Multnomah Publishers, 2000), p. 31.

4. Crabb, Larry, *Shattered Dreams* (Colorado Springs: Waterbrook Press, 2010), p. 144.

5. Jones, Robert D, "Conflict: When Desires Become Demands," Crossway, 2012, https://www.crossway.org/articles/conflict-when-desires-become-demands/.

6. Piper, John, "God Is Always Doing 10,000 Things in Your Life," Desiring God, 2013, https://www.desiringgod.org/articles/god-is-always-doing-10000-things-in-your-life.

7. Marcoux, Heather, "Millennial Dads Spend Three Times as Much Time With Their Kids Than Previous Generations." Mother.ly, 2018, https://www.mother.ly/parenting/millennial-dads-spend-more-time-with-their-kids/.

8. Keller, Timothy, *The Reason for God: Belief in an Age of Skepticism* (New York City: Penguin Books, 2008), p. 234.

9. Greig, Pete, *God on Mute: Engaging the Silence of Unanswered Prayer* (Grand Rapids: Regal Books, 2007), p. 227.

CHAPTER 4

1. Lewis, C. S., *A Grief Observed* (New York: Harper & Row, 1989), p. 25.

2. Lewis, C. S., *A Grief Observed* (San Francisco: Harper & Row, 1989), p. 1.

3. Yancey, Phillip, *The Jesus I Never Knew* (Zondervan Publishing House, 1995), p. 358.

4. *The Apostle*, directed by Robert Duvall, October Films, 1997.

CHAPTER 5

1. O'Connor, Mary Francis, *The Grieving Brain* (HarperOne, 2022), p.7.

CHAPTER 6

1. Wallace, David Foster, "Why What We Value Defines Our Personal Identity," The Right Questions, accessed May 2024, https://therightquestions.co/tag/david-foster-wallace/.

2. Bruce, F.F., *The Gospel of John: Introduction, Exposition, and Notes* (Grand Rapids: Eerdmans, 1983).

3. Piper, John, "Faith and the Imputation of Righteousness," Desiring God, October 1999, https://www.desiringgod.org/messages/faith-and-the-imputation-of-righteousness.

4. Holcomb, Justin, Lindsey, *Rid of My Disgrace* (Wheaton: Crossway, 2011), p. 15.

5. Manning, Brennan, *The Ragamuffin Gospel: Good News for the Bedraggled, Beat-Up, and Burnt Out* (Colorado Springs: Multnomah Publishers, 2000), p. 3.

CHAPTER 7

1. Wilson Jr., Stephen, "Twisted," *Son of Dad*, Big Loud Records, 2023.

2. Bruce, F.F., *The Gospel of John: Introduction, Exposition, and Notes* (Grand Rapids: Eerdmans, 1983).

3. Spurgeon, Charles, *The New Park Street Pulpit,* vol. 6 (Grand Rapids: Baker House Books, 1990), "A Basket Full of Summer Fruit."

4. Spurgeon, Charles, "Quotable Quotes," Princeofpreachers.org, accessed May 2024, https://www.princeofpreachers.org/quotable-quotes.html.

5. Eareckson Tada, Joni, "Knowing and Loving the Bible episode 05," Journeywomen, accessed August, 2024 33 min., 42 sec, https://www.journeywomen.org/episode/promises-of-gods-word.

6. Groeschel, Craig, *Hope in the Dark* (New York City: HarperCollins Publishing, 2018), p. 23.

7. *The Shawshank Redemption*, directed by Frank Darabont, Columbia Pictures, 1994.

8. Keller, Timothy, *The Reason For God: Belief in an Age of Skepticism* (New York City: Penguin Books, 2008), p. 234.

9. Hillsong United, "Highlands: Song of Ascent," *People*, Hillsong Music and Capitol Christian Music Group, 2019.

10. Houdmann, Michael, "What are the Different Names of God and What do They Mean?" Got Questions, accessed April 2024, https://www.gotquestions.org/names-of-God.html.

11. Piper, John, "Every Promise is Yes in Him," Sovereign Grace Worship Conference, Lousiville, KY, 2024.

12. Henry, Matthew, *The Communicant's Companion* (Birmingham: Solid Ground Christian Books, 2005), p. 130.

13. KingsPorch, "Faithful Still," *God Is In The House*, BEC Recordings, 2023.

CHAPTER 8

1. Chung, Daisy, "Talking Trees." *National Geographic*, vol. 233 no. 6, 2018.

2. Nouwen, Henri, *Out of Solitude* (South Bend: Ave Maria Press, 2004), p. 38.

3. Stott, John,*The Cross of Christ* (InterVarsity Press, 2012), p. 266.

4. Tripp, Paul, *Lead: 12 Gospel Principles for Leadership in The Church* (Wheaton: Crossway, 2020), p. 12.

5. "Our Epidemic of Loneliness and Isolation," accessed April 2024, https://www.hhs.gov/sites/default/files/surgeon-general-social-connection-advisory.pdf.

6. *Grumpy Old Men*, directed by Donal Petrie, Warner Brothers, 1993.

CHAPTER 9

1. Brontë, Emily, *Wuthering Heights 7th edition* (New York City, Penguin Publishing, 2012).

2. Spurgeon, Charles, "Job's Resignation." Delivered at the Metropolitan Tabernacle, March 11, 1886.

3. Piper, John, "Embrace The Life God Has Given You." Desiringgod.org, March 10, 2017, https://www.desiringgod.org/embrace-the-life-god-has-given-you.

4. Beuchner, Frederick, *A Crazy, Holy Grace.* (Grand Rapids: Zondervan, 2017), p. 58.

5. Springer, Rita, "Trials of Many Kinds." *Fed By Ravens*, Our Records, 2024.

6. "50 Quotes from Tim Keller," Tgc.org, May 19, 2023, TheGospel Coalition/article/50-quotes-tim-keller/?amp=1.

7. Bolen, Zach & Brian Eichelberger, "Heaven Is in Our Sights," Fear, Humble Beast, 2019.

8. Lloyd-Jones, Sally, *Jesus Storybook Bible* (Grand Rapids: Zonderkids, 2007), p. 347.

Grieving the Loss of Those Whose Eternities Were Uncertain

A TIME
TO MOURN

WILL DOBBIE

978-1-5271-1067-0

A Time to Mourn

Grieving the Loss of Those Whose Eternities Were Uncertain

Will Dobbie

To a Christian, the death of an unbeliever is heartbreaking. But even in the darkness of grief, there can be light. Will Dobbie's nuanced examination of the hope found in the Bible offers more than shallow comfort.

The death of unbelieving loved ones is a taboo. Often we don't know how to grieve, or how to comfort Christian friends who have experienced that loss. Where do we find hope when all seems hopeless? The answer is in the character of the God who reveals Himself in the pages of Scripture.

With the tone of a pastor, who knows how hard it is to lose an apparently unbelieving friend, Will Dobbie directs our eyes towards the One who alone knows for certain the destiny of the departed. He points us to the God who, in the case of the lost, shares our heartache and comforts us, the God who is loving and compassionate as well as just and holy and wise. Ultimately, he shows us the God who is glorious.

Christian Focus Publications

Our mission statement
Staying Faithful

In dependence upon God we seek to impact the world through literature
faithful to His infallible Word, the Bible. Our aim is to ensure that the
Lord Jesus Christ is presented as the only hope to obtain forgiveness of
sin, live a useful life and look forward to heaven with Him.

Our Books are published in four imprints:

◁○✕ CHRISTIAN FOCUS

Popular works including biographies, commentaries, basic doctrine and
Christian living.

◁○✕ MENTOR

Books written at a level suitable for Bible College and seminary students,
pastors, and other serious readers. The imprint includes commentaries,
doctrinal studies, examination of current issues and church history.

◁○✕ CHRISTIAN HERITAGE

Books representing some of the best material from the rich heritage
of the church.

◁○✕ CF4KIDS

Children's books for quality Bible teaching and for all age groups:
Sunday school curriculum, puzzle and activity books; personal and
family devotional titles, biographies and inspirational stories –
because you are never too young to know Jesus!

Christian Focus Publications Ltd,
Geanies House, Fearn, Ross-shire,
IV20 1TW, Scotland, United Kingdom.
www.christianfocus.com